Witness

Contents

Bearing False Witness

Jimmy Carter's PALESTINE PEACE NOT APARTHEID

CAMERA Monograph Series

A publication of CAMERA,
Committee for Accuracy in Middle East Reporting in America
Boston, Massachusetts

Bearing False
Jimmy Carter's
PALESTINE
PEACE NOT APARTHEID

CAMERA, the Committee for Accuracy in Middle East Reporting in America, is a national media-monitoring organization founded in 1982 that works to promote more accurate, balanced and complete coverage of Israel and the Middle East. Aware of the vital role of the mass media in shaping public perception and public policy, CAMERA seeks to educate both journalists and news consumers about the complex issues related to achievement of peace in the Middle East. CAMERA is a non-profit, tax-exempt organization under section 501(c)(3) of the United States Internal Revenue Code.

Published by
The Committee for Accuracy in Middle East Reporting in America
CAMERA
P.O. Box 35040
Boston, MA 02135

ISBN 0-9661548-3-2

Photo Credits: P. 9 Keystone/Getty Hulton Archive, P. 11 Tsuni/Gamma, P. 13 Mike Theiler/Reuters, P. 16 Adel Hana/AP, P. 18 (top) Nancy Kaszerman/Zuma Press, (bottom) Washington Institute, P. 19 Mohamad Torokman/Reuters, P. 21 (top) Uriel Sinai, (bottom) Reinhard Krause/Reuters, P. 22 Israel Government Press Office, P. 24 Mohamed Zatari/AP, P. 25 Gianangelo Pistoia/AP, P. 26–27 (top) Ministry of Foreign Affairs Web site, P. 28 Mohammad Kheirkhah/UPI, P. 30 Amos Ben Gershom Govt Press Office, P. 37 Ric Feld/AP, P. 40 Emory University, P. 45 (top) Kevin Dietsch/UPI, (bottom) Arthur Grace/Zuma Press, P. 47 Israel Government Press Office, P. 50 Getty Hulton Archive, P. 58 CNN, P. 61 Apollo Images/Gamma, P. 69 Brian Snyder, P. 87 Roslan Rahman/Agence France Presse, P. 88 Ahmed Jadallah/Reuters, P. 91 Rabih Moghrabi/Agence France Presse

Book design by Susan Rubin

Executive Summary

Jimmy Carter's *Palestine: Peace Not Apartheid* set off a firestorm when it appeared in the fall of 2006, with critics noting the many false, incendiary and often ludicrous charges against Israel leveled by, of all people, an ex-president of the United States. Another former president, Bill Clinton, told a San Diego audience: "It's not factually correct and it's not fair."[1] The *New Republic's* Martin Peretz called the volume "a tendentious, dishonest and stupid book."[2] Slate's Michael Kinsley headlined his commentary: "It's Not Apartheid: Jimmy Carter's Moronic New Book About Israel."[3] *The New York Times'* Ethan Bronner termed it "a strange little book,"[4] skewed against Israel.

A cascade of resignations from the Carter Center in Atlanta, including that of Professor Kenneth Stein, its first executive director, signaled further repudiation of the work and its author.

The outcry had little apparent effect, though, on Carter and his publisher, Simon and Schuster, with neither indicating that any of the material errors and other shortcomings would be addressed—save one about poor wording. Carter unblushingly denied problems in his book, literally laughing at and ridiculing his critics when, for instance, challenged by a CNN anchor on specific distortions. In Op-Eds and on the airwaves, he touted the perfect accuracy of the book and blamed the so-called Israel lobby and Jewish organizations for any negative reaction.

Simon and Schuster and its publisher, David Rosenthal, likewise took no responsibility for the countless factual inaccuracies in this ostensibly non-fiction work. "Do we check every line in every book? No, but that's not the issue here. I have no reason to doubt Carter's research," he said. "We stand by the book fully," Rosenthal declared.[5]

Carter's many falsehoods, in fact, echo crude anti-Israel propaganda—as the title's "apartheid" misnomer makes obvious. While little in the book itself invokes the South Africa analogy directly, Carter does argue the apartheid epithet fits Israel's treatment of the Palestinians. The motives are not racially based, he contends, but concern settlements and the construction of what he calls the "segregation wall," which have together created "forced separation" allegedly aimed at "the acquisition of land." The ex-president offers a muddle of erroneous and distorted allegations and anecdotes about the barrier, West Bank roads and settlements to cast Israel as oppressive and brutish. Entirely unmentioned are, for example, the details and dimensions of the onslaught of Palestinian terrorist infiltrations from the West Bank into Israeli towns and cities that prompted building the security barrier—and the dramatic effects the structure has had in helping reduce death and injury.

The term "Apartheid," of course, defines only institutional racism, nothing else; the loaded book title was meant to shock, to smear Israel with the worst accusation of the day whether relevant or not. Such is the shoddiness and mendacity of the entire book.

Among the most insistently reiterated and fundamentally false allegations made are those that relate to the historical record and key agreements. In multiple passages in his book and in many interviews given while promoting it, Carter charges Israel with violating international law and the will of the international community. He claims formal and agreed-upon borders have existed since 1967, coinciding with the 1949 armistice lines that define the West Bank. He claims United Nations Security Council Resolution 242 required Israel to retreat to these lines and yield the territory of the West Bank to the Palestinians and that in not doing so Israel has flouted the law and world opinion. He argues that this is the primary cause of persisting conflict.

In fact, none of this is true. The 1949 cease-fire lines do not constitute internationally recognized borders between Israel and the West Bank; Resolution 242 purposely refrained from insisting on Israeli return to the armistice lines and instead called for the negotiation of "secure and recognized boundaries"; and as recent concessions by Israel suggest, conflict is rooted in a broader Arab rejection of Israel's legitimate exsistence.

Carter claims he intended with his book to foster debate about the Arab-Israeli conflict, but this too is fakery. With the acquiescence of universities and other communal groups sponsoring his lectures, he has successfully used his status to duck nearly all direct engagement with critics in public venues. Speaking to scores of thousands at universities across America, he has uttered one uncontested false, inflammatory statement after another, all the while claiming to be a peacemaker.

Only members of the media have had opportunity to confront him as he has made the rounds of television and radio plugging *Palestine: Peace Not Apartheid.* In these settings, he has at times encountered challenges and several of those exchanges have been telling. Among these was a brief interview on a Denver radio station in which Carter bluntly denied that then Hamas Prime Minister Ismail Haniyeh had just publicly declared in a statement in Teheran his refusal ever to recognize Israel's legitimacy. Although the facts were obvious and unequivocal, Carter insisted Haniyeh had not made the statement. That segment was suggestive of the often surreal divergence from indisputable facts that characterizes the ex-president's arguments as a whole—both in his book and in his appearances.

It also underscores Carter's obvious ill will toward Israel and its Jewish citizens, an animosity that is especially expressed in his disregarding, downgrading and denying genuine threats to the people and the nation. Terrorism against Israel is only minimally noted. The vast anti-Semitic hate campaigns of the Arab world, purveyed in media, mosques and schools, and the ongoing calls for Israel's destruction, are omitted. Rather, Israel's self-declared, mortal enemies are warmly extolled as reasonable and decent. In one anecdote after another, Carter repeats their grievances against Israel, whether uttered by dictators and hereditary potentates or terrorist chieftains, whether by Hafez al Assad, Yasir Arafat or various Saudis, Jordanians and Palestinians.

Arafat evokes especially warm words from Carter, who writes: "In 1969 the PLO found a strong leader in Yasir Arafat, a well-educated Palestinian who was the head of al-Fatah, a guerilla organization. As chairman, Arafat turned much of his attention to raising funds for the care and support of the refugees and inspiring worldwide contributions to their cause." Arafat, in reality, "turned much of his attention" to terrorist activity against Israel and directed "contributions" to his own accounts and those of his inner circle, leaving many of his people in poverty.

Revealing too is the ten-page "Historical Chronology" in *Palestine: Peace Not Apartheid,* beginning with Abraham and including various regional and related events in the modern era, up to August, 2006. Carter inserts entries for 1939 and 1947 but neglects to mention the Holocaust. That is, his list of "important events that have led to the existing state of affairs" omits the Nazi annihilation of one third of the Jewish people.

As to why the ex-president harbors such extreme animus, many have noted his bias is consistent with longstanding and close friendships with Arab rulers, some of whom lavishly fund the Carter Center. (While Carter is relentless in scrutinizing and faulting Israel for its alleged infractions, his Center is virtually silent about the grave abuse of human rights in Arab states.) Likewise, commentators have considered the religious dimension of his own brand of Christianity and his apparent conflating of a particularly harsh and anti-Jewish interpretation of the Hebrew Bible with a jaundiced perspective on modern Israel.

Whatever his motives—religious, political, personal—there is little doubt that even a one-term president dramatically rejected by voters carries the prestige of the most powerful office in the world. His obsessive attacks on Israel, predicated on an array of absurd and propagandistic claims, have to be systematically countered.

This volume reviews many of the material errors made in the book and often repeated in interviews and other writing. It includes articles by a number of expert analysts who examine Carter's policies, statements and perspectives. Kenneth Stein, Dennis Ross, Michael Oren, Alan Dershowitz, Melvin Konner and Rachel Ehrenfeld are among the contributors who offer important insight about the former president's lamentable distortions.

At a time when Israel faces biased political attacks, even in places like Britain and Norway (often fueled by chronic media misinformation), there is an urgent need to assure that defamatory falsehoods do not also poison Americans' understanding of Middle East realities. Jimmy Carter's screed is an opportunity to restate essential facts and also to underscore the need for reform of reckless publishing houses, such as Simon and Schuster, that violate basic standards of accuracy, while promoting and profiting from such "non-fiction" books.

Andrea Levin
Executive Director, CAMERA

1. *The Jewish Daily Forward,* March 30, 2007.
2. The Spine, A *New Republic* Blog, November 14, 2006.
3. Slate, December 11, 2006.
4. *The New York Times,* January 7, 2007.
5. *The New York Times,* December 7, 2006.

Chapter 1

Factual Errors in *Palestine: Peace Not Apartheid*

Falsehoods and More Falsehoods

Chief among the myriad defects of Jimmy Carter's book is the fundamental problem of its many factual errors concerning the Arab-Israeli conflict—errors related to historical events, international agreements, national policies and recent occurrences. Identifying these many inaccurate statements and refuting them serves to highlight the fallacious underpinnings of Carter's overall analysis, in particular his gross mischaracterizations of the actions of Israel and that nation's adversaries, and the false premises of his prescriptions for achieving peace.

Despite widespread criticism of the factual shoddiness of *Palestine: Peace Not Apartheid,* Carter has regularly boasted in press appearances and lectures of the allegedly pristine accuracy of his book. In an appearance on "Larry King Live" on Nov. 27, 2006, for instance, he insisted: "Everything in the book, I might say, is completely accurate."

In the *Los Angeles Times* (December 8, 2006), he declared: "I used maps, text and documents to describe the situation accurately and to analyze the only possible path to peace..."

In an interview with Tavis Smiley (December 11, 2006), he insisted: "The book is absolutely true, and it tells about the horrible, almost unbelievable abuse of Palestinians in their own land, where the land has been occupied, confiscated, and then colonized by the occupying powers."

He told CNN's Soledad O'Brien on December 13, 2006: "I know what I'm talking about and the book is completely accurate."

In the *Washington Post* (January 18, 2007), he declared that "most critics have not seriously disputed or even mentioned the facts ..."

In reality, of course, much of the criticism of the book has focused on its pervasive and serious misrepresentations of fact. Moreover, Carter has frequently reiterated the same falsehoods and distortions proffered in the book in television, radio, and print appearances, as well as for numerous audiences at bookstores, college campuses, symposia and other venues.

Following is a review of many of the factual errors in *Palestine: Peace Not Apartheid* along with some of Carter's false statements made in the media and elsewhere, mainly while promoting the book. The list is not comprehensive; it would be virtually impossible to cite every inaccurate or distorted statement made in the book and in the author's public appearances. The errors cited are organized by category.

INTERNATIONAL AGREEMENTS AND BORDERS

Carter continually misrepresents the contents of peace agreements, peace proposals and U.N. Security Council Resolution 242, then falsely casts Israel as violating the letter and spirit of international law and betraying American administrations and the world community in general. Thus, for instance, Carter writes on page 208, in a concluding chapter, that: "The overriding problem is that, for more than a quarter century, the actions of some Israeli leaders have been in direct conflict with the official policies of the United States, the international community, and their own negotiated agreements."

Errors Concerning UN Resolution 242

CARTER:

Palestine: Peace Not Apartheid, Page 38: "...U.N. Resolution 242, which confirmed Israel's existence within its 1949 borders."

Palestine: Peace Not Apartheid, Page 215: "[An option for Israel is] withdrawal to the 1967 border specified in U.N. Resolution 242 and as promised in the Camp David Accords and the Oslo Agreement..."

PBS NewsHour, November 28, 2006: "The demand is for them [the Israelis] to give back all the land. The United Nations resolutions that apply, the agreements that have been made at Camp David under me and later at Oslo for which the Israeli leaders received the Nobel Peace Prizes, was based [sic] on Israel's withdrawal from occupied territories."

Canadian Broadcasting Corporation, December 8, 2006: "It's a minority of Israeli leaders who prefer to occupy Palestinian land that is the obstacle to peace. It's a violation of United Nations resolutions. It's a violation of the agreements that were worked out at Camp David. It's a violation of the agreement that Israeli leaders and Parliament accepted in Oslo because of the Norwegians. It's a violation of the international Quartet's Road Map, all of which call for Israel to withdraw from occupied territories."

FACT:

All the agreements Carter cites are predicated on U.N. Security Council Resolution 242 and none—the Camp David Accords, the Oslo Accords, the Road Map—requires Israel to "give back all the land" and return to the vulnerable pre-1967 armistice lines. Nor in its continuing presence in the West Bank is Israel in "violation" of the agreements cited.

Resolution 242 calls on Israel to withdraw from territory in the context of negotiations that assure the "right to live in peace within secure and recognized boundaries free from threats or acts of force."[1] Despite many efforts, peace summits and signed accords there has yet to be a conclusive agreement defining "secure and recognized boundaries."

"In a number of speeches at the U.N. in 1967, I repeatedly stated that the armistice lines fixed after 1948 were intended to be temporary." —Arthur Goldberg

"Had we said that you must go back to the 1967 line, which would have resulted if we had specified a retreat from all the occupied territories, we would have been wrong." —Lord Caradon

Britain's Lord Caradon, (left) chief architect of U.N. Resolution 242 and America's Ambassador Arthur Goldberg (right) at the United Nations.

And, contrary to the ex-President, UNSCR 242 does not specify the extent of Israel's withdrawal from the West Bank. The drafters of 242 repeatedly, explicitly and emphatically spelled out their reasoning. For example, Lord Caradon, the chief architect of the resolution, observed:

> We could have said: well, you go back to the 1967 line. But I know the 1967 line, and it's a rotten line. You couldn't have a worse line for a permanent international boundary. It's where the troops happened to be on a certain night in 1948. It's got no relation to the needs of the situation. Had we said that you must go back to the 1967 line, which would have resulted if we had specified a retreat from all the occupied territories, we would have been wrong.
>
> In New York, what did we know about Tayyibe and Qalqilya? If we had attempted in New York to draw a new line, we would have been rather vague. So what we stated was the principle that you couldn't hold territory because you conquered it, therefore there must be a withdrawal to—let's read the words carefully—"secure and recognized boundaries." They can only be secure if they are recognized. The boundaries have to be agreed; it's only when you get agreement that you get security. I think that now people begin to realize what we had in mind—that security doesn't come from arms, it doesn't come from territory, it doesn't come from geography, it doesn't come from one side dominating the other, it can only come from agreement and mutual respect and understanding.[2]

Lord Caradon reiterated the argument on a 1978 PBS segment:

> We didn't say there should be a withdrawal to the '67 line; we did not put "the" in, we did not say all the territories deliberately. We all knew that the boundaries of '67 were not drawn as permanent frontiers, they were a cease-fire line of a couple of decades earlier.... We did not say that the '67 boundaries must be forever.[3]

Errors Concerning "Borders"

In conjunction with many of the distortions about 242, Carter continually injects inaccurate references to Israel's supposedly established and internationally recognized eastern "borders" along the West Bank. However, no such borders have ever been finalized. The Camp David Accords, signed by Carter himself, state: "The negotiations [concerning the West Bank and Gaza] will resolve, among other matters, the location of the boundaries ...." The Oslo Agreements deferred "borders" as one of the "issues that will be negotiated in the permanent status negotiations" (Article XVII, 1, a). Similarly, the Road Map of 2003 invokes 242 and states that a "process" would begin in 2004 "leading to a final, permanent status resolution in 2005, including on borders, Jerusalem, refugees, settlements."

Carter continually injects inaccurate references to Israel's supposedly established and internationally recognized eastern "borders" along the West Bank.

No permanent status resolution on these issues has yet occurred.

CARTER:

Palestine: Peace Not Apartheid, Page 57: "The 1949 armistice demarcation lines became the borders of the new nation of Israel and were accepted by Israel and the United States, and recognized officially by the United Nations."

Palestine: Peace Not Apartheid, Page 190: "[Israel's security barrier] is projected to be at least three and a half times as long as Israel's internationally recognized border..."

Palestine: Peace Not Apartheid, Page 207: "The unwavering official policy of the United States since Israel became a state has been that its borders must coincide with those prevailing from 1949 until 1967 (unless modified by mutually agreeable land swaps) .... Also as a member of the International Quartet that includes Russia, the United Nations, and the European Union, America supports the Roadmap for Peace, which espouses exactly the same requirements."

Palestine: Peace Not Apartheid, Page 216: "The bottom line is this: Peace will come to Israel and the Middle East only when the Israeli government is willing to comply with international law, with the Roadmap for Peace, with official American policy, with the wishes of a majority of its own citizens—and honor its own previous commitments—by accepting its legal borders."

Tavis Smiley Show, PBS, December 11, 2006: "...twenty-three Arab countries agreed to recognize Israel's right to exist in peace inside their legal borders... But that's not something that Israel is willing to accept, to live inside their own borders. The international borders."

In an interview with Tavis Smiley, pictured right, Carter claimed: "...twenty-three Arab countries agreed to recognize Israel's right to exist in peace inside their legal borders...But that's not something that Israel is willing to accept, to live inside their own borders. The international borders."

Lecture at George Washington University, March 7, 2007: "Condoleezza Rice has called for early U.S.-Israeli-Palestinian peace talks. She recommended, by the way, as a basis for peace, the 2002 offer of all 23 Arab nations—that is, full recognition of Israel, based on a return to its internationally recognized borders. And this recommendation is compatible with all U.S. official policy of our government since before I became president and since, also is compatible with United Nations resolutions and also with previous agreements which the Israeli government has approved overwhelmingly in 1978, as I've already mentioned, and later, in 1993, with the Oslo agreement."

FACT:
The 1949 armistice lines separating the West Bank from Israel never became permanent borders recognized by Israel, the United States or the U.N. Security Council. Israel's only internationally recognized borders are those between Israel and Egypt and Israel and Lebanon. Indeed, the Jordanian-Israeli General Armistice Agreement of April 3, 1949 specifically notes that the lines are not borders: "The Armistice Demarcation Lines defined in articles V and VI of this Agreement are agreed upon by the Parties without prejudice to future territorial settlements or boundary lines or to claims of either Party relating thereto." Nor, obviously, was there any "unwavering official policy," as Carter alleges, defining Israel's eastern "borders."

President Johnson said on June 19, 1967: "The nations of the region have had only fragile and violated truce lines for 20 years. What they now need are recognized boundaries and other arrangements that will give them security against terror, destruction, and war."

Arthur Goldberg, the U.S. ambassador to the United Nations from 1965-1968, explained in a March 12, 1980 letter to the *New York Times:* "In a number of speeches at the U.N. in 1967, I repeatedly stated that the armistice lines fixed after 1948 were intended to be temporary."

Errors Concerning Camp David

CARTER:
Palestine: Peace Not Apartheid, Pages 51-52: ...[I]mportant provisions of our [1978/79] agreement have not been honored since I left office. The Israelis have never granted any appreciable autonomy to the Palestinians ...

FACT:

Obviously, after 1993 the Palestinians gained "appreciable autonomy." The Oslo process created the Palestinian Authority, giving Palestinians control of political, civic, security, medical, educational and media institutions. Under the Accords, Israel ceded 40 percent of the West Bank, and unilaterally pulled out from Gaza entirely. About 98 percent of the Palestinian population lived in the areas of Palestinian self-rule. Any subsequent Israeli military incursions into these areas have been in response to their use by Palestinians as bases for terrorism.

With regard to Palestinian autonomy and the original Camp David agreements, Carter grossly distorts the facts. Efforts to negotiate details of an autonomy agreement failed then not because of Israel, but because Yasir Arafat and his lieutenants publicly denounced such efforts and any Palestinians who supported them were killed.

For example, the *New York Times* reported on a Christian Palestinian from Ramallah who had publicly rejected the PLO in favor of seeking peace via the path of Begin and Sadat. "Defying the PLO," by *Times'* senior editor John Oakes (December 21, 1977) told of Abdel-nur Khalil Janho, who was said to be:

> ... typical of those Palestinian Arabs of the West Bank who have no use for the PLO's extreme position and terrorist tactics, who fear its radicalism and who do not accept the dogma that it is in fact the sole legitimate representative of the Palestinian people. ... this position, rarely expressed openly by Arabs in the occupied territories prior to the Sadat peace initiative, has suddenly come alive not only with Mr. Sadat's downgrading of the PLO, but especially since President Carter stated that moderate Palestinians now must be included in the discussions at the Cairo conference, which the PLO has rejected.

According to Mr. Janho,

> the Sadat-Begin approach now gives a unique opportunity for the 750,000 West Bank Arabs to be liberated from the occupation and at the same time help along in the process of reconciliation by holding out a friendly hand to the Israelis. And if this opportunity isn't made the most of by the Arabs who live inside the West Bank, the PLO outside will again seize the initiative, the whole peace effort will collapse and the radicals will take over.

Questioned by Oakes about the many West Bank mayors who supported the PLO, Janho replied,

> they were elected at a time when West Bank Arabs could see no possibilities of a peaceful settlement with the Israelis ... but all that's changed now, as a result of Sadat. There is an alternative to [the] PLO; we have a chance to regain our identity and our dignity without war. Petitions in support of Mr. Sadat's moves, signed by 9,000 Arab citizens of Nablus, the West Bank's largest city and center of PLO sentiment, would seem to bear him out.

Regrettably, however, only a few weeks later a PLO hit-squad gunned down Mr. Janho.

Shortly after the *Times* story, the PLO press agency WAFA announced on December 26, 1977 that orders had been given to "liquidate a number of agents,"

With regard to Palestinian autonomy and the original Camp David agreements, Carter grossly distorts the facts. Efforts to negotiate details of an autonomy agreement failed then not because of Israel, but because Yasir Arafat and his lieutenants publicly denounced such efforts and any Palestinians who supported them were killed.

Jimmy Carter (left front) and Israel's Aharon Barak (right front) at a September 2003 symposium commemorating the 1978 Camp David Accords. Barak's account of the negotiations vindicated Israeli Prime Minister Menahem Begin, accused by Carter of betraying agreement on a settlement freeze.

and on that very day the PLO announced in Beirut its responsibility for the murder of Hamdi Kadi, a Palestinian resident of Ramallah who was willing to work with the Israelis. According to the *Washington Post,* "The announcement of Kadi's assassination followed a PLO statement rejecting Israel's latest proposals for limited Arab self-rule on the West Bank." (December 27, 1977)

Ironically, Carter was to become an advisor, friend and advocate of Yasir Arafat, even though it was the PLO leader who undermined Camp David's autonomy components and whose minions liquidated courageous moderates who embraced the president's proposals. In his reflexive blaming of Israel and whitewashing of the PLO's role regardless of the facts, as illustrated in this episode, Carter reveals his sharp bias against the Jewish state.

CARTER:
Palestine: Peace Not Apartheid, Page 50: "Perhaps the most serious omission of the Camp David talks was the failure to clarify in writing Begin's verbal promise concerning the settlement freeze during subsequent peace talks."

Washington Post Op-Ed, Nov. 26, 2000: "Prime Minister Begin pledged that there would be no establishment of new settlements until after the final peace negotiations were completed. But later, under Likud pressure, he declined to honor this commitment ...."

FACT:

Menahem Begin promised in the Camp David discussions to maintain a three month settlement freeze and he adhered to his commitment. This was dramatically underscored in a public forum about the Camp David agreements on September 17, 2003 at the Woodrow Wilson Center. A member of the panel, Israeli jurist Aharon Barak, explained he had attended the relevant meeting at which the settlement freeze discussion transpired, had been the only one present taking notes, and that his notes showed Begin had agreed only to a three month freeze.

In the background, Carter is heard to state, "I don't dispute that." William Quandt then added that while he had not been in the meeting, Secretary of State Cyrus Vance had, and told him immediately afterwards that Begin had agreed to a three month freeze, but they hoped to get it lengthened the next day. Neither Carter, nor Barak, nor Quandt indicated that Begin had ever agreed to extend the freeze.

Throughout Carter's formulations, the Palestinians are, regardless of the facts, cast as near perfect in both fealty to agreements and to the cause of peace, while Israel is condemned for violating both.

Errors Concerning the Road Map

In a pattern apparent throughout Carter's formulations, the Palestinians are, regardless of the facts, cast as near perfect in fealty both to agreements and to the cause of peace, while Israel is condemned for violating both.

CARTER:

Palestine: Peace Not Apartheid, Page 173: "[Abbas and his key advisers] pointed out that Palestinian leaders had accepted all provisions of the Quartet's Roadmap for Peace, but that Sharon had publicly rejected most of its key provisions. There was no doubt that Abbas had the support and respect of his people and was dedicated to the immediate pursuit of a peace agreement in accordance with the Roadmap."

Palestine: Peace Not Apartheid, Page 187: "He [Abbas] has publicly endorsed the international community's Roadmap for Peace without equivocation and has been eager to negotiate with Israel since first becoming prime minister three years before being elected president."

Palestine: Peace Not Apartheid, Page 207: "Palestinian leaders unequivocally accepted this proposal, but Israel has officially rejected its key provisions with unacceptable caveats and prerequisites."

CNBC, The Tim Russert Show, Dec. 2, 2006: "[The Road Map peace plan] was immediately adopted in its totality by the Palestinians, who still have no caveats and no objections to the Road Map terms."

FACT:

Mahmoud Abbas did, indeed, verbally express his support for the June 2003 document. But there is no evidence that the Palestinian Authority cabinet or parliament ever approved the Road Map, as would be required for such an international agreement. Indeed, there's no evidence it was ever even discussed by these bodies. Nor was Abbas clearly "dedicated" to achieving an "agreement in accordance with the Road Map."

He attached caveats to PA implementation of the Road Map. He insisted, for example, that Palestinian prisoners be released before he would take any required steps, even though prisoners were not mentioned in the agreement. He also flatly ruled out taking forcible action to disarm and dismantle the infrastructure of terror, saying he would rely on persuasion alone; Abbas thus flouted the most essential Palestinian commitment to the agreement and to achieving a stable peace. Violence against Israelis actually increased almost immediately after the signing of the Road Map. On June 11, 2003, Hamas blew up a bus in Jerusalem, killing 17 and wounding 100.

Regarding Ariel Sharon's response to the U.S. initiative, American officials made clear at the outset they expected feedback from the parties. A statement by Secretary of State Colin Powell and National Security Advisor Condoleezza Rice on May 23, 2003 underscored this:

> The roadmap was presented to the Government of Israel with a request from the President that it respond with contributions to this document to advance true peace. The United States Government received a response from the Government of Israel, explaining its significant concerns about the roadmap.
>
> The United States shares the view of the Government of Israel that these are real concerns, and will address them fully and seriously in the implementation of the roadmap to fulfill the President's vision of June 24, 2002.

Despite concerns, the Israeli Cabinet promptly endorsed the plan. As *Ha'aretz* reported on May 25, 2003:

> ...the Israeli cabinet formally approved the U.S.-backed road map for an Israeli-Palestinian settlement yesterday. The cabinet approved the map—a three-phase plan that calls for a settlement freeze and an end to terror attacks in the first stage, a Palestinian state with temporary borders in the second and a final-status agreement by 2005—by a vote of 12-7, with four abstentions, at the end of a stormy six-hour debate...

Errors Concerning U.N. Resolution 425 and Lebanon

Carter misrepresents the facts regarding Israel's complete withdrawal from Lebanon in the spring of 2000, a withdrawal certified by the United Nations.

Carter misrepresents the facts regarding Israel's complete withdrawal from Lebanon in the spring of 2000, a withdrawal certified by the United Nations. Echoing allegations of some Arab groups, including Hezbollah, Carter claims Israel has not completely withdrawn from Lebanon.

CARTER:

Palestine: Peace Not Apartheid, Page 71: Israel has relinquished its control over ... almost all of Lebanon ...

Palestine: Peace Not Apartheid, Page 98: [A number of events influenced] Israel's decision in May 2000 to withdraw almost completely from Lebanon after eighteen years of occupation, retaining its presence only in Shebaa Farms.

FACT:
Israel did not "withdraw *almost completely*" from Lebanon. On June 16, 2000, United Nations Secretary General Kofi Annan reported to the Security Council that "Israeli forces have withdrawn from Lebanon in compliance with resolution 425" and "in compliance with the line of withdrawal identified by the United Nations."

(Security Council Resolution 425 called on Israel to "withdraw forthwith its forces from all Lebanese territory." The line identified by the United Nations "conform[ed] to the internationally recognized boundaries of Lebanon based on the best available cartographic and other documentary material.")

Two days later, the Security Council endorsed the Secretary General's conclusion that Israel had withdrawn from all Lebanese territory.

Errors Concerning U.N. Resolution 1701 and Hezbollah

CARTER:
Palestine: Peace Not Apartheid, Page 200: "Finally, on August 11, the United Nations Security Council passed resolution 1701, which provided that combat would cease and that 15,000 Lebanese troops and an equal number from the international community would be deployed in Southern Lebanon as both Israeli and Hezbollah military forces withdrew. *The key issues of prisoner exchange ... and the disarming of Hezbollah were postponed ...*" (emphasis added)

FACT:
In fact, an operative paragraph of UNSC Resolution 1701 calls for "full implementation of the relevant provisions of the Taif Accords, and of resolutions

Carter wrongly claimed Resolution 1701 "postponed" the "disarming of Hezbollah" gunmen such as those above.

1559 (2004) and 1680 (2006), that require the disarmament of all armed groups in Lebanon, so that, pursuant to the Lebanese cabinet decision of 27 July 2006, there will be no weapons or authority in Lebanon other than that of the Lebanese State."

And the third paragraph of the resolution emphasizes the need for an "unconditional release of the abducted Israeli soldiers," while the fourth paragraph also encourages "the efforts aimed at urgently settling the issue of the Lebanese prisoners detained in Israel."

MISREPRESENTING PEACE PROPOSALS, NEGOTIATIONS, AND OTHER INITIATIVES

Aggression against Israel and Arab recalcitrance are erased, and Israel is then blamed for failing to be forthcoming or, alternatively, for not responding to fictitious peace offers.

Carter regularly falsifies the facts about negotiations, peace efforts and other initiatives. Aggression against Israel and Arab recalcitrance are erased, and Israel is then blamed for failing to be forthcoming or, alternatively, for not responding to fictitious peace offers. For instance, Carter charges Israel did not make a generous offer at the 2000/2001 Camp David/Taba talks, one that "any Palestinian leader could accept." He also emphatically insists Israel did not endorse the far-reaching proposals put forth by President Clinton. Likewise he disregards the actual contents of the 2006 so-called prisoners' proposal by Palestinians and recasts it as entailing acceptance of Israel. He has also rewritten the facts about the implacable Hafez Al Assad to claim Assad was ready for an agreement with Israel.

Camp David/Taba Negotiations

CARTER:

Palestine: Peace Not Apartheid, Pages 150-51: "Later, during his last months in Washington, President Clinton made what he called his final proposal. Eighty percent of Israeli settlers would remain in the West Bank, and Israel could maintain its control of the Jordan River valley … .

"There was no clear response from Prime Minister Barak, but he later stated that Israel had twenty pages of reservations. President Arafat rejected the proposal. …

"The best offer to the Palestinians—by Clinton, not Barak—had been to withdraw 20 percent of the settlers, leaving more than 180,000 in 209 settlements, covering about 10 percent of the occupied land, including land to be 'leased' and portions of the Jordan River valley and East Jerusalem."

CNN, The Situation Room, Nov. 28, 2006: "You could check with all the records. Barak never did accept [the Clinton parameters]."

CNBC, The Tim Russert Show, Dec. 2, 2006: "The fact is that the proposals [Clinton] made were never accepted by either Barak on behalf of the Israelis or by the Palestinians' Arafat."

FACT:
Carter gets both the terms of the proposals and the responses of the Israelis and Palestinians wrong. For instance, according to Clinton's parameters, Israel would not "maintain its control of the Jordan Valley" as it had in the past. The proposal entailed "a small Israeli presence" under the authority of an international force that could remain in "fixed locations" but that would withdraw after a maximum of 36 months. Israel would withdraw from "between 94 and 96 percent of West Bank territory" and there would be a land swap of 1 to 3 percent.

Israeli Prime Minister Ehud Barak's response was clear—he accepted the parameters, as Dennis Ross, the chief U.S. negotiator, described in *The Missing Peace,* his definitive account of those discussions. Ross has also reiterated the facts in interviews since Carter's book appeared. In a December 8, 2006 segment on CNN's "Situation Room with Wolf Blitzer," there was the following exchange:

CNN's Wolf Blitzer (top) and Middle East peace negotiator Dennis Ross

> **Blitzer:** Who is right, Jimmy Carter or Bill Clinton on this question which is so relevant as to whether or not the Israelis at Camp David at the end of the Bill Clinton administration accepted the proposals the U.S. put forward?
>
> **Ross:** The answer is President Clinton. The Israelis said yes to this twice. First at Camp David there were a set of proposals that were put on the table that they accepted. And then were the Clinton parameters, the Clinton ideas which were presented in December. Their government, meaning the cabinet, actually voted it. You can go back and check it, December 27th the year 2000, the cabinet voted to approve the Clinton proposal, the Clinton ideas. So this is—this is a matter of record. This is not a matter of interpretation.
>
> **Blitzer:** So you're saying Jimmy Carter is flat wrong.
>
> **Ross:** On this issue, he's wrong.

CARTER:
Palestine: Peace Not Apartheid, Page 148: Maps on this page are labeled: "Palestinian Interpretation of Clinton's Proposal 2000" and "Israeli Interpretation of Clinton's Proposal 2000."

FACT:
The maps are mislabeled. Dennis Ross, the U.S. peace negotiator who drew up the original version of Carter's maps, explained:

> The problem is that the "Palestinian interpretation" is actually taken from an Israeli map presented during the Camp David summit meeting in July 2000, while the "Israeli interpretation" is an approximation of what President Clinton subsequently proposed in December of that year. Without knowing this, the reader is left to conclude that the Clinton proposals must have been so ambiguous and unfair that Yasir Arafat, the Palestinian leader, was justified in rejecting them. But that is simply untrue.[4]

Prisoners' Proposal

CARTER:

Palestine: Peace Not Apartheid, Page 214: "The prisoners' proposal called for a unity government with Hamas joining the PLO, the release of all political prisoners, acceptance of Israel as a neighbor within its legal borders ..."

FACT:

While calling for a Palestinian state in the West Bank and Gaza Strip, the so-called prisoners' proposal, formulated by Palestinians without any involvement of Israel, says nothing about "acceptance of Israel as a neighbor." Many Palestinian leaders have emphasized that the document entails no recognition of Israel whatsoever.

Abdul Rahman Zidan, a Palestinian government minster from Hamas's "Change and Reform" list, told the BBC: "You will not find one word in the document clearly stating the recognition of Israel as a state."[5]

Hamas leader Khalil Abu Leila said that "Fatah wants from us more than what is in this document. They want Hamas to recognize Israel and be a copy of Fatah, something that will not happen.... We will never recognize Israel."[6]

Salah Bardaweel, the leader of the Hamas faction in parliament, said: "We accept a state in [territory occupied] in 1967, but we did not say we accept two states."[7]

Contrary to Carter's claims about the so-called prisoners' proposal, Hamas official Abdul Rahman Zidan (right) denied the document entailed any recognition of Israel.

Syria's Assad and Negotiations

CARTER:

Palestine: Peace Not Apartheid, Page 130: "...when I visited Damascus in 1990, President Assad informed me that he was willing to negotiate with Israel on the status of the Golan Heights. His proposal was that both sides withdraw from the international border ... [and] Syria might move its troops farther from the border because of the terrain."

FACT:

Former executive director of the Carter Center Kenneth Stein, who participated in the meeting with Carter and Assad, explained in a *Los Angeles Times* article that:

> his own notes of the Damascus meeting show that Assad, in response to a question from Carter, replied that Syria could not accept a demilitarized Golan without "sacrificing our sovereignty." Stein also disputed Carter's statement in the book that Assad expressed willingness to move Syria's troops farther from the border than Israel should be required to do.[8]

ERRORS CONCERNING ISRAEL'S SECURITY BARRIER

Much of Carter's commentary about the security barrier Israel erected as a defense against unprecedented terrorism originating from the West Bank echoes extreme anti-Israel propaganda. He terms the barrier an "imprisonment wall,"[9] a "segregation wall"[10] and a "segregation barrier;"[11] claims its purpose is "the acquisition of land"[12] and grossly misrepresents its location. He includes only passing and oblique mention of the actual purpose of the barrier in reducing death and destruction in Israel by Palestinian infiltrators. In the briefest of sanitized terms, he notes, for instance, that Israel drew lessons about the utility of constructing a barrier from the fence already built around Gaza, which had led to "a substantial decrease in *cross-border raids.*"[13] Obviously, "cross-border raids" conveys little about the reality of terrorists murdering civilians. (And, of course, there's the misnomer in citing a "border.")

Likewise, he refers to "Israeli *arguments* that the wall is to keep Palestinian suicide bombers from Israel,"[14] as though Israel had contrived the excuse of terrorist infiltrators to launch its callous building project and as though the lives saved and attacks prevented were undocumented and debatable. Nearly a thousand Israelis had been murdered in terrorist attacks and thousands more injured in a span of three years beginning in September 2000, an onslaught that led to erecting the barrier. Within the first year, when significant portions were completed, the incidence of attacks had declined by nearly 90%. The book contains no data about the sharp reduction in deaths and injuries to Israelis. Nor is there any reference whatever to the bomb factories and terror-training in West Bank towns that spawned attackers who crossed sometimes within minutes into Israel to blow up Israeli civilians in buses, cafes and at religious events. The barrier is portrayed as one more gratuitous and cruel policy of a monstrously selfish Israel.

The book contains no data about the sharp reduction in deaths and injuries to Israelis. The barrier is portrayed as one more gratuitous and cruel policy of a monstrously selfish Israel.

Carter all but omits the Palestinian terrorist onslaught against Israel and the suffering inflicted on Israelis, young and old.

CARTER:

Palestine: Peace Not Apartheid, Page 189: "Their presumption is that an encircling barrier will finally resolve the Palestinian problem. Utilizing their political and military dominance, they are imposing a system of partial withdrawal, encapsulation, and apartheid on the Muslim and Christian citizens of the occupied territories. The driving purpose for the forced separation of the two peoples is unlike that in South Africa—not racism but the acquisition of land."

Palestine: Peace Not Apartheid, Page 190: "The governments of Ariel Sharon and Ehud Olmert have built the fence and wall entirely within Palestinian territory, intruding deeply into the West Bank to encompass Israeli settlement blocs and large areas of other Palestinian land."

CNBC, The Tim Russert Show, Dec. 2, 2006: "And this wall, unlike the Berlin Wall, which was built on East German territory, none of this wall is built on Israeli territory. It's all built inside the West Bank .... And in no place along that wall does it separate Palestinians from Israelis to protect Israelis. Everywhere the wall separates Palestinians from other Palestinians."

CSPAN2, Book TV, Dec. 3, 2006: "... this wall is not built between Palestinian land and Israeli land. No place does the wall touch Israel. The wall is entirely inside Palestine. And the wall is designed as it's presently planned and being built completely inside Palestine not to protect Israelis but to take Palestinian land, and all you have to do is look at a map ... it shows the route of the wall."

Israel's Security Barrier—mostly fence, not wall—has helped to reduce sharply terrorist infiltrations from the West Bank.

Contrary to Carter's contention that "in no place along that wall does it separate Palestinians from Israelis" but rather separates Palestinians from Palestinians—the barrier is situated between Israelis and Palestinians along most of its path.

Tavis Smiley Show, PBS, December 11, 2006: "In every inch of it, it separates Palestinian land from from other Palestinian land. And it's not designed to protect Israelis from Palestinian attacks...What it's designed to do is to take away Palestinian land and that's what I'm trying to reveal in this book."

University of California, Berkeley, May 2, 2007: "In some cases [the wall] completely surrounds a city. For Qalia (sic) which is up in the northern part of the West Bank is wholly surrounded by a fence. It's well inside Palestinian territory... Bethlehem is completely surrounded by wall deep inside the West Bank."

FACT:
Carter's many assertions about the path and purpose of the barrier are totally spurious and divorced from reality. United Nations maps and numbers confirm that the barrier adheres to the "green line"—the armistice line marking the boundaries of the West Bank—along about 140 km (45 percent) of the green line's path. Contrary to Carter's obsessively-repeated and absurd contention that "in no place along that wall does it separate Palestinians from Israelis" but rather separates Palestinians from Palestinians—the barrier is situated between Israelis and Palestinians along most of its path.

Moreover, in some places the barrier also veers into Israeli territory. (For example, near Tulkarm and Al Mughayyir Al Mutilla.)

Carter's statements at Berkeley about Qalquilya are totally deceptive and distorted. Indeed, the town is essentially surrounded by the barrier because geographically it juts into Israel; it is not "well inside Palestinian territory" but the opposite. It directly abuts the Green Line on its western side and is adjacent to the Israeli city of Kfar Sava. Because of shooting by Palestinian gunmen from the Arab town into Israel, the wall is concrete in this stretch. Carter is equally inaccurate in describing Bethlehem. There the barrier curves along the northern half of the city, from which multiple suicide bombers have come. Bethlehem is not "completely surrounded."

CARTER:
Palestine: Peace Not Apartheid, Page 190: [The barrier] is projected to be at least three and a half times as long as Israel's internationally recognized border ...

FACT:
The United Nations Office for the Coordination of Humanitarian Affairs notes that "Because of its meandering path into the West Bank, the [total 703 km length of the route] is more than twice the length of the "Green Line"—315 km."

MINIMIZING AND OMITTING ANTI-ISRAEL VIOLENCE AND ARAB REJECTIONISM

One of the most striking features of Carter's book is the near total omission of reference to the hatred and aggression directed against Israelis and Jews by Arab states and groups. A chronology of historical events omits Arab aggression in the 1930's as well as during the decades of international terrorism against Israelis and others that made aircraft hijacking and suicide bombing synonymous with the Palestinian cause. Israel's extreme adversaries, including those advocating the nation's destruction, are cast as benign and reasonable. Demonization of Jews in the media, mosques and political discourse of the Arab world is omitted completely. The net effect is to frame Israeli actions taken in self-defense against aggression as irrationally violent and those of Arafat, Hafez al Assad, Hamas, Hezbollah and other Arab actors as harmless and reasonable.

Yasir Arafat with Jimmy Carter, who embraced the PLO leader as a friend.

Whitewashing Arafat and Hamas

CARTER:

Palestine: Peace Not Apartheid, Page 62: When I met with Yasir Arafat in 1990, he stated, "The PLO has never advocated the annihilation of Israel. The Zionists started the 'drive the Jews into the sea' slogan and attributed it to the PLO."

FACT:

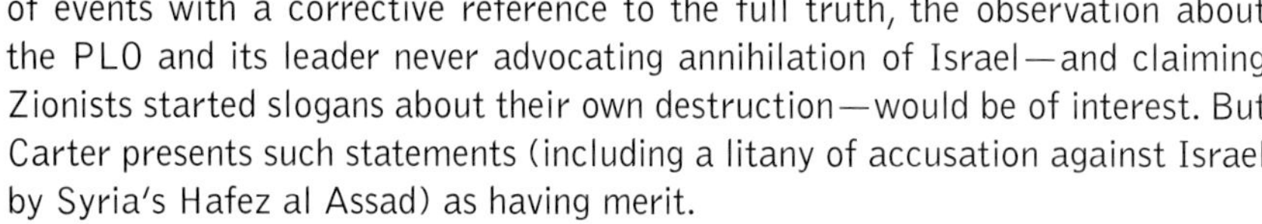
Were Carter to present Arafat's bizarre statement as a point of departure for exploring the man's view of events with a corrective reference to the full truth, the observation about the PLO and its leader never advocating annihilation of Israel—and claiming Zionists started slogans about their own destruction—would be of interest. But Carter presents such statements (including a litany of accusation against Israel by Syria's Hafez al Assad) as having merit.

The Palestinian cause as expressed by Arafat and the PLO is rooted in the goal of destroying Israel. The founding PLO charter speaks almost exclusively of "the liberation of Palestine" and calls on Palestinians to "move forward on the path of jihad until complete and final victory has been attained." (This was written in 1964, before Israel controlled the West Bank and Gaza Strip. Liberating "Palestine" referred not only to these areas but to all the territory between the Jordan River and the Mediterranean Sea—including Israel.) It adds: "The partitioning of Palestine, which took place in 1947, and the establishment of Israel are illegal and null and void ..."

Likewise, the 1968 version of the charter describes "Palestine" as the area encompassing the West Bank, Gaza Strip and Israel, then states: "Armed struggle is the only way to liberate Palestine. This is the overall strategy, not merely a tactical phase."

Arafat himself frequently called for destroying Israel. An extensive interview in the March 29, 1970 *Washington Post* with famed journalist Oriana Fallaci contains multiple such statements, including:

> We shall never stop until we can go back home and Israel is destroyed.
>
> The goal of our struggle is the end of Israel, and there can be no compromises or mediations. Whether our friends like it or not, the dimensions of our struggle will always remain those outlined by the principles of Al Fateh: First, revolutionary violence is the only means for the liberation of the land of our forefathers; second, the goal of this violence is the elimination of Zionism from Palestine in all its political, economic and military aspects...
>
> We don't want peace; we want victory. Peace for us means Israel's destruction and nothing else.

Similar statements appear through the decades as in "[p]eace for us means the destruction of Israel. We are preparing for an all-out war, a war which will last for generations" (*El Mundo* [Venezuela], Feb. 11, 1980). Arafat also regularly called for Jihad against Israel[15] and promoted the so-called phased plan to destroy Israel.[16]

And, contrary to Carter/Arafat, Arabs had long invoked the image of throwing the Jews into the sea. A *New York Times* column by Flora Lewis on April 10, 1988 recounted that Ahmed Shukairy, a founder of the PLO, had, "preached holy war at the Great Mosque in East Jerusalem the Friday before the Six-Day war began, promising to 'throw the Jews into the sea.'"

More recently, Lieutenant-Colonel Munir Maqdah, who had commanded Arafat's Fatah army in Lebanon before being suspended, said his forces would continue fighting "the Jews and their agents" despite any peace talks, promising that "[s]ooner or later we will throw the Zionists into the sea." (Reuters, Oct. 8, 1993)

In an interview with Italian journalist Oriana Fallaci, Arafat repeatedly called for the destruction of Israel.

CARTER:

Palestine: Peace Not Apartheid, Page 179: "Hamas was now [January 2006] holding many local posts, and their incumbent officials had been free of any allegations of corruption and, for sixteen months, had meticulously observed a cease-fire commitment, which they called hudna."

Palestine: Peace Not Apartheid, Page 184: "When I questioned him about the necessity for Hamas to renounce violence and recognize Israel, [Hamas member Dr. Mahmoud Ramahi] responded that

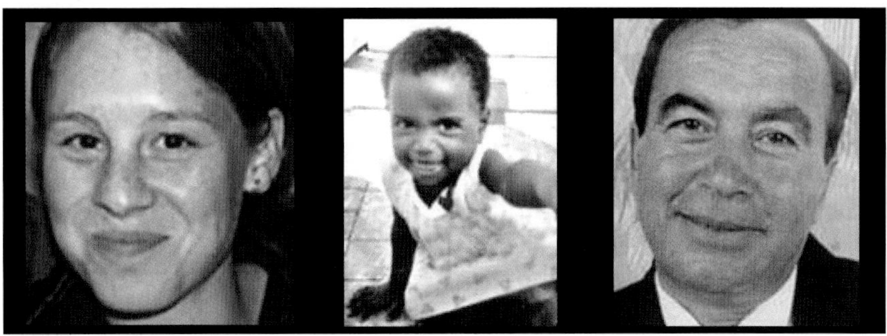

Among the civilian Israelis murdered by Hamas during the period in which Carter claims the group had "meticulously observed a cease-fire" and "not a single" life was lost are (left to right) Dana Galkowicz 22, Dorit Benisian 2, Herzl Shlomo 51, Ofer Tiri 23, Oded Sharon 36, Yuval Abebeh, 4.

they had not committed an act of violence since a cease-fire was declared in August 2004 ..."

CNN, Larry King Live, Nov. 27, 2006: "... since August of 2004 ... Hamas has not been guilty of an act of terrorism that cost an Israeli life."

PBS, NewsHour, November 28, 2006: Carter: "... since August of 2004, Hamas has not committed a single act of terrorism that cost an Israeli life, not a single one."

Canadian Broadcasting Corporation, December 8, 2006: "You have to look at the facts. That is, take Hamas, for instance, the number one organization that is accused. There hasn't been an Israeli life lost from Palestinian terrorism—that is Hamas—since August of 2004. They imposed unilaterally a cease-fire, which they call a hudna."

Tavis Smiley Show, PBS, December 11, 2006: "...almost a year and a half ago, Hamas declared a unilateral cease-fire. They call it a 'hudna.' And there hasn't been a single Israeli killed with a Hamas terrorist attack since August of 2004."

FACT:

At least a dozen Israeli civilians were murdered by Hamas members during the period in which, according to Carter's repeated statements, the group had "meticulously" observed a cease-fire and had not "committed a single act of terrorism that cost an Israeli life, not a single one."

On Sept. 29, 2004, two preschool children, Yuval Abebeh, 4, and Dorit Benisian, 2, were killed by a Qassam rocket fired from Gaza into the Israeli town of Sderot. Hamas claimed responsibility.

One of the most striking features of Carter's book is the near total omission of reference to the hatred and aggression directed against Israelis and Jews by Arab states and groups.

On October 6, 2004, a 24 year-old greenhouse worker, Pratheep Nanongkham, was killed by a Hamas terrorist.

On January 2, 2005, 25 year-old Nissim Arbiv was killed in a Hamas attack while working at the Erez Industrial Park.

On Jan 13, 2005, Palestinian terrorists attacked the Karni crossing between the Gaza Strip and Israel, killing 6 civilians. The victims were Dror Gizri, 30, of Sderot; Ibrahim Kahili, 46, of Umm al-Ghanem; Munam Abu Sabia, 33, of

Daburiyeh; Ivan Shmilov, 53, of Sderot; Herzl Shlomo, 51, of Sderot; and Ofer Tiri, 23, of Ashkelon. Hamas claimed joint responsibility.

On July 14, 2005, Dana Galkowicz, 22, was killed by a Qassam rocket fired from Gaza into Israel. Hamas claimed responsibility.

On September 21, 2005, Sasson Nuriel, 55, was kidnapped and murdered. Hamas claimed responsibility.

Moreover, in addition to the Hamas killings, scores more Israelis were murdered by Islamic Jihad, the Popular Front for the Liberation of Palestine, Al Aqsa Martyrs Brigades and other groups.

CARTER:
In a dramatic instance of Carter's extreme efforts to deny reality, he argued with a radio interviewer who confronted him with a current example of Hamas Prime Minister Ismail Haniyeh reiterating the group's rejection of Israel's legitimacy and existence. The exchange went as follows:

KHOW-AM, The Caplis & Silverman Show (Denver), Dec. 12, 2006:

> **Silverman:** Didn't the head of Hamas, the elected leader of the Palestinians, go to Tehran last week and say, "We will never recognize the usurper Zionist government ..."
>
> **Carter:** No, he didn't.
>
> **Silverman:** ... and we will continue our jihad-like movement ...
>
> **Carter:** No, he didn't do that.
>
> **Silverman:** until the liberation of Jerusalem?
>
> **Carter:** No, he didn't do that. I saw no report about that.

When radio host Craig Silverman confronted Carter on the air about Hamas's recent extreme anti-Israel statements the ex-president simply denied the facts.

Craig Silverman, KHOW-AM radio.

FACT:

Many media outlets reported the statements of Haniyeh. The *International Herald Tribune,* for instance, carried an Associated Press account on December 8, 2006 whose essentials were similarly cited as well by many other newspapers and electronic media:

"Haniya soundly rejected such steps as he addressed thousands of worshipers at Tehran University. The United States and Israel, he said, 'want us to recognize the usurpation of the Palestinian lands and stop jihad and resistance and accept the agreements reached with the Zionist enemies in the past.'"

He added: "We will never recognize the usurper Zionist government and will continue our jihad-like movement until the liberation of Jerusalem."

Haniya said the policy of not recognizing Israel was "irreversible."

CARTER:

Palestine: Peace Not Apartheid, Page 8: "1996: Palestinians elect Yasir Arafat as president and elect the members of a legislative council. Israelis return the Likud Party to power, which stalls the Oslo process."

Hamas leader Ismail Haniyeh in Tehran with Iran's Mahmoud Ahmadinejad.

"We will never recognize the usurper Zionist government and will continue our jihad-like movement until the liberation of Jerusalem."
—Ismail Haniyeh

FACT:
In a chronology of events, Carter distorts cause and effect, omitting entirely the milestone terror attacks by Palestinians in February and March 1996 that killed 60 Israelis and derailed the Oslo process. As Reuters reported on March 3, 1996, "After last Sunday's Hamas bombings killed 26 people, [Labor leader Shimon] Peres lost a commanding lead in opinion polls."

CARTER:
Palestine: Peace Not Apartheid, Page 145: "Of 1,696 voting places outside Jerusalem [during the 1996 Palestinian elections], there were problems in only two. Three Palestinians were shot and killed by Israeli police at a checkpoint at Jenin ..."

FACT:
Here Carter makes a gross error of omission. The Associated Press, *New York Times,* Agence France Press and others reported at the time that the Palestinians at the checkpoint were killed after opening fire on Israeli security forces. According to the *Boston Globe* on January 21, 1996, an Israeli soldier was wounded when the three—all Hamas members—"tried to shoot their way past an Israeli roadblock."

ISRAELI POLICIES AND MILITARY ACTIONS

In many passages, Carter makes false and derogatory references to Israel, whether in his recalled conversation with Hafez al Assad, who is said to have lamented Israeli racism and injustice, or in various baseless charges related to Israel's treatment of Palestinians, its participation in hostage negotiations and its actions in the Hezbollah war of 2006.

Land and Water Issues

CARTER:
Palestine: Peace Not Apartheid, Page 168: "Living among 1.3 million Palestinians, the 8,000 Israeli settlers [in the Gaza Strip] were controlling 40 percent of the arable land and more than one-half the water resources ..."

FACT:
Settlers lived on roughly 15-20 percent of Gaza land, and controlled little of its water. In fact, Israel supplied, and continues to supply, large amounts of water to Palestinians in the Gaza Strip.

The American Journalism Review in August/September 2004 published the following correction after similarly mis-stating Gaza statistics: "In 'Caught in the Crossfire' (June/July 2004), Barbara Matusow wrote that Israeli settlers occupy 25 percent of the land in the Gaza Strip and control most of the water resources. According to the Institute of Applied Research in Jerusalem, the Palestinians control 95 percent of the water resources in Gaza. Estimates vary widely when it comes to control of the land, however. A June 2004 report on Gaza by the World Bank states that 15 to 20 percent of the land is occupied by settlements."

CARTER:
Palestine: Peace Not Apartheid, Page 121: "Each Israeli settler uses five times as much water as a Palestinian neighbor, who must pay four times as much per gallon."

FACT:
According to Sharif Elmusa, who was a water negotiator for the Palestinian side in talks with Israel, Palestinians in the West Bank pay approximately $1 per cubic meter for domestic water, "virtually identical with the price in Israel ..."[17] While both Arab and Jewish Israelis use more water per capita than Palestinians, the ratio is just half of what Carter claims.[18]

Similarly, with regard to agricultural water, Elmusa writes: " ... in absolute terms, the price of irrigation water in Israel, the West Bank, and Jordan converged, and water prices could not have affected competitiveness in any significant way."[19]

In fact, some Palestinians—those in Jericho, Tulkarm and Gaza—have paid substantially less for water than the typical Israeli household.

Israel's Supreme Court building

CARTER:
Palestine: Peace Not Apartheid, Page 151: "There is a zone with a radius of about four hundred meters around each settlement within which Palestinians cannot enter."

CARTER:
Not only do Palestinians routinely enter within four hundred meters of Israeli settlements, they frequently enter into the settlements. For example, Palestinians from villages near the Israeli settlement of Ariel work alongside Israelis at a textile factory in the settlement.

Interrogation Legalities

CARTER:
Palestine: Peace Not Apartheid, Page 197: "Confessions extracted through torture are admissible in Israeli courts."

Under Israeli criminal procedures, when a person claims that his confession was extracted via torture, a "trial-within-a-trial" is immediately held in which the prosecution must prove that torture or other illegitimate means were not used.

FACT:
Under Israeli criminal procedures, when a person claims that his confession was extracted via torture, a "trial-within-a-trial" is immediately held (in Hebrew mishpat zuta) in which the prosecution must prove that torture or other illegitimate means were not used. If the prosecution is unable to disprove claims of torture the confession is thrown out. In addition, if it appears that other illegal means short of torture were used, the confession can be admitted, but only if the court finds that the interrogation did not prejudice the defendant's free will.[20]

Gilad Shalit kidnapping

Typical of factual errors that minimize Israeli vulnerability and denigrate the nation's efforts to cope with violence is Carter's account of the June 2006 kidnapping of Gilad Shalit and killing of two Israeli soldiers in Israel by Palestinians from Gaza. He neglects to mention the killings, then misrepresents the Palestinians' terms for a prisoner swap and wrongly claims Israel "rejected any negotiations."

CARTER:
Palestine: Peace Not Apartheid, Page 197: "The cycle of violence erupted once more in June 2006, when Palestinians dug a tunnel under the barrier that surrounds Gaza and attacked some Israeli soldiers, capturing one of them. They offered to exchange the soldier for the release of 95 women and 313 children who are among some 8,500 Palestinians in Israeli prisons. Israel rejected any negotiations..."

CSPAN2, Book TV, December 3, 2006: "... And what the Palestinians asked for is, 'We'll swap you this one soldier [Gilad Shalit] if you'll just release some of the hundred women you're holding—about a hundred—or some of the little children you're holding ...,' and the Israeli government refused to swap ...."

FACT:
On June 26, 2006, CNN reported: "Palestinian militants distributed a statement Monday saying they will provide ***information*** about a kidnapped Israeli soldier if Israel agrees to release all female prisoners and all children under 18 being held in Israeli jails." (Emphasis added.)

Israel's *Ha'aretz* newspaper on July 12, 2006 subsequently reported: "For its part, Hamas is demanding that 400 prisoners be freed in the first part of the deal, and 500 each in the two subsequent parts of the exchange. Israel would like to limit that figure. However, a senior Israeli source said this week that it is possible that Israel will agree to the release of as many as 1,000 Palestinians." According to the same *Ha'aretz,* story, one of the prisoners Hamas demanded Israel release is "Abbas Sayed, the mastermind of the massacre at the Park Hotel in Netanya over Passover in 2002, in which 29 civilians were killed."

A January 3, 2007 *Jerusalem Post* story reported: "A senior Hamas official said Thursday his group was ready to give Israel a videotape of the soldier if it agreed to release Palestinian women prisoners and other detainees." The article suggests the videotape-prisoner swap would be prelude to a further exchange. Ahmed Youssef, political advisor to Palestinian Authority Prime Minister Ismail Haniyeh, "claimed that Israel had agreed to release 200 prisoners who had been sentenced to long prison terms, including senior officials from Hamas and other Palestinian factions."

Finally, regarding Carter's charge that Israel holds over 300 Palestinian "children" or "little children", it's not clear exactly what age he is referring to, but in 1967, under Jordan and Egypt, the "age of criminal responsibility" in the West Bank and Gaza was nine. Israel raised it to 12, and rarely if ever prosecutes any children under the age of 14.[21] Thus, even according to Palestinian statistics, as of July 2005 there was just one detainee between the ages of 12 and 13, and three between the ages of 13 and 14; the largest number by far, 130, were at least 17 years old. In 2006, also according to Palestinian statistics, no children 14 years or younger were sentenced by Israel. To put these ages in context, it should be noted that in the PA under Article 67 of the Palestinian Child Law, the age of criminal responsibility is just nine, while in Mr. Carter's home state of Georgia, where he served as governor, the age is as low as 13 for serious crimes.

Hezbollah War

CARTER:

Palestine: Peace Not Apartheid, Page 201: "What were the causes and results of the Israeli-Lebanese war? The conflict began when Hezbollah militants attacked two Israeli vehicles, killing three soldiers and capturing two others. ...Israel ...surprisingly declared that it had been assaulted by the entire nation of Lebanon, and launched an aeriel bombardment ..."

FACT:

Carter omits mention that the attack was in Israel, and Hezbollah fired rockets across northern Israel as part of the assault, one of them scoring a direct hit on a home and wounding four. As far as his surprise that Israel held Lebanon responsible, Hezbollah was a key member of the Lebanese government, and that government's Policy Guidelines stated support for Hezbollah's attacks against Israel: "Protection of [Hezbollah] and recognition that it is a genuine Lebanese manifestation of our right to liberate our lands from any occupation." Notwithstanding Hezbollah's political role in Lebanon, Israel confined its retaliation to Hezbollah strongholds and left unscathed most of the nation.

---

1. United Nations Security Council Resolution 242, November 22, 1967
The Security Council,
Expressing its continuing concern with the grave situation in the Middle East,
Emphasizing the inadmissibility of the acquisition of territory by war and the need to work for a just and lasting peace in which every State in the area can live in security,
Emphasizing further that all Member States in their acceptance of the Charter of the United Nations have undertaken a commitment to act in accordance with Article two of the Charter,

> *Affirms* that the fulfillment of Charter principles requires the establishment of a just and lasting peace in the Middle East which should include the application of both the following principles:

Withdrawal of Israeli armed forces from territories occupied in the recent conflict;

Termination of all claims or states of belligerency and respect for and acknowledgement of the sovereignty, territorial integrity and political independence of every State in the area and their right to live in peace within secure and recognized boundaries free from threats or acts of force;

Affirms further the necessity

For guaranteeing freedom of navigation through international waterways in the area;

For achieving a just settlement of the refugee problem;

For guaranteeing the territorial inviolability and political independence of every State in the area, through measures including the establishment of demilitarized zones;

Requests the Secretary General to designate a Special Representative to proceed to the Middle East to establish and maintain contacts with the States concerned in order to promote agreement and assist efforts to achieve a peaceful and accepted settlement in accordance with the provisions and principles in this resolution;

Requests the Secretary-General to report to the Security Council on the progress of the efforts of the Special Representative as soon as possible.

2. *Journal of Palestine Studies,* "An Interview with Lord Caradon," Spring-Summer 1976, pp. 144-145.

3. The MacNeil-Lehrer Report, March 30, 1978

4. *New York Times,* January 9, 2007

5. *Philadelphia Inquirer,* June 28, 2006

6. *Boston Globe,* June 29, 2006

7. *Chicago Tribune,* June 29, 2006

8. *Los Angeles Times,* January, 17, 2006

9. *Palestine: Peace Not Apartheid,* page 174.

10. Ibid, page 191.

11. Ibid, page 192.

12. Ibid, page 190.

13. Ibid, page 190.

14. Ibid, page 194.

15. *Yediot Ahronot,* October 23, 1996: "We know only one word—jihad. jihad, jihad, jihad. Whoever does not like it can drink from the Dead Sea or from the Sea of Gaza."

16. Radio Monte Carlo, September 1, 1993: "[The Oslo agreement] will be a basis for an independent Palestinian state in accordance with the Palestinian National Council resolution issued in 1974 ... The PNC resolution issued in 1974 calls for the establishment of a national authority on any part of Palestinian soil from which Israel withdraws or which is liberated."

17. Sharif S. Elmusa, *Water Conflict: Economics, Politics, Law and Palestinian-Israeli Water Resources,* page 144.

18. Statistical Abstract of Israel, 1996.

19. Elmusa, page 173.

20. See for example, *The Right to a Fair Trial,* D. Weissbrodt and R. Wolfrum, eds., Springer, 1997.

21. Human Rights in the Administered Areas, Justus Reid Weiner, Wisconsin International Law Journal, Vol. 10, No. 2, Spring 1992, pp 221-222

22. Palestinian Political Child Prisoners in Israeli Prison—Monthly Update Until 5 of July 2005, Child and Youth Department, Ministry of Detainees and Ex-Detainees Affairs; http://www.edrp.gov.ps/CYD/CYD%20Report%20705.pdf.

23. Palestinian Child Political Prisoners: 2006 Report, Defence for Children International Palestine Section; http://www.dci-pal.org/english/doc/Reports/2007/ChildPrisoners2006.doc

24. Dealing with alleged child collaborators in the Occupied Palestinian Territories in the spirit of the Convention on the Rights of the Child, 20 April 2005, Defence for Children International—Palestine Section; http://www.dci-pal.org/english/doc/reports/2005/jun11.pdf

25. Georgia Transfer Provisions, State Juvenile Justice Profiles, National Center for Juvenile Justice; http://www.ncjj.org/stateprofiles/asp/transfer.asp?topic=Transfer&state=GA06.asp&print=no

Don't Play With Maps

by Dennis Ross

I became embroiled in a controversy with former President Jimmy Carter over the use of two maps in his recent book, *Palestine Peace Not Apartheid.* While some criticized what appeared to be the misappropriation of maps I had commissioned for my book, *The Missing Peace,* my concern was always different.

I was concerned less with where the maps had originally come from — Mr. Carter has said that he used an atlas that was published after my book appeared — and more with how they were labeled. To my mind, Mr. Carter's presentation badly misrepresents the Middle East proposals advanced by President Bill Clinton in 2000, and in so doing undermines, in a small but important way, efforts to bring peace to the region.

In his book, Mr. Carter juxtaposes two maps labeled the "Palestinian Interpretation of Clinton's Proposal 2000" and "Israeli Interpretation of Clinton's Proposal 2000."

The problem is that the "Palestinian interpretation" is actually taken from an Israeli map presented during the Camp David summit meeting in July 2000, while the "Israeli interpretation" is an approximation of what President Clinton subsequently proposed in December of that year. Without knowing this, the reader is left to conclude that the Clinton proposals must have been so ambiguous and unfair that Yasir Arafat, the Palestinian leader, was justified in rejecting them. But that is simply untrue.

In actuality, President Clinton offered two different proposals at two different times. In July, he offered a partial proposal on territory and control of Jerusalem. Five months later, at the request of Ehud Barak, the Israeli prime minister, and Mr. Arafat, Mr. Clinton presented a comprehensive proposal on borders, Jerusalem, Palestinian refugees and security. The December proposals became known as the Clinton ideas or parameters.

Put simply, the Clinton parameters would have produced an independent Palestinian state with 100 percent of Gaza, roughly 97 percent of the West Bank and an elevated train or highway to connect them. Jerusalem's status would have been guided by the principle that what is currently Jewish will be Israeli and what is currently Arab will be Palestinian, meaning that Jewish Jerusalem — East and West — would be united, while Arab East Jerusalem would become the capital of the Palestinian state.

The Palestinian state would have been "nonmilitarized," with internal security forces but no army and an international military presence led by the United States to prevent terrorist infiltration and smuggling. Palestinian refugees would have had the right of return to their state, but not to Israel, and a fund of $30 billion would have been created to compensate those refugees who chose not to exercise their right of return to the Palestinian state.

"It is certainly legitimate to debate whether President Clinton's proposal could have settled the conflict. It is not legitimate, however, to rewrite history and misrepresent what the Clinton ideas were."

—Dennis Ross

When I decided to write the story of what had happened in the negotiations, I commissioned maps to illustrate what the proposals would have meant for a prospective Palestinian state. If the Clinton proposals in December 2000 had been Israeli or Palestinian ideas and I was interpreting them, others could certainly question my interpretation. But they were American ideas, created at the request of the Palestinians and the Israelis, and I was the principal author of them. I know what they were and so do the parties.

It is certainly legitimate to debate whether President Clinton's proposal could have settled the conflict. It is not legitimate, however, to rewrite history and misrepresent what the Clinton ideas were.

Indeed, since the talks fell apart, there has emerged a mythology that seeks to defend Mr. Arafat's rejection of the Clinton ideas by suggesting they weren't real or they were too vague or that Palestinians would have received far less than what had been advertised. Mr. Arafat himself tried to defend his rejection of the Clinton proposals by later saying he was not offered even 90 percent of the West Bank or any of East Jerusalem. But that was myth, not reality.

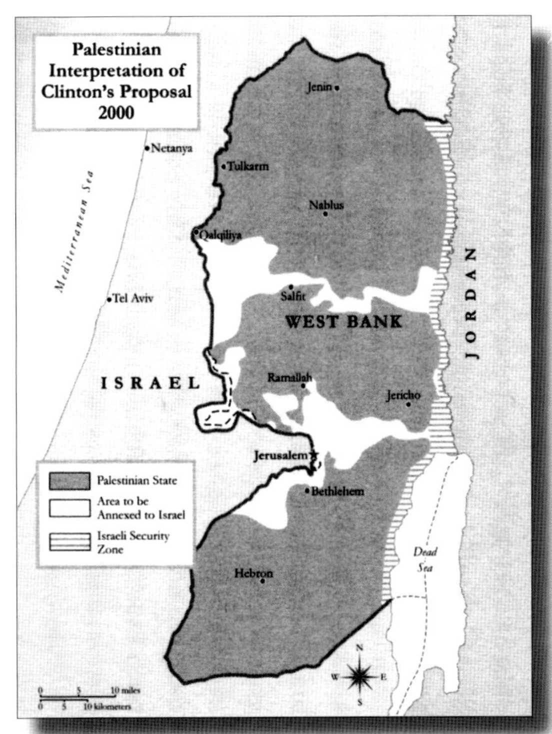

Carter's mislabeled maps

Why is it important to set the record straight? Nothing has done more to perpetuate the conflict between Arabs and Israelis than the mythologies on each side. The mythologies about who is responsible for the conflict (and about its core issues) have taken on a life of their own. They shape perception. They allow each side to blame the other while avoiding the need to face up to its own mistakes. So long as myths are perpetuated, no one will have to face reality.

And yet peace can never be built on these myths. Instead it can come only once the two sides accept and adjust to reality. Perpetuating a myth about what was offered to justify the Arafat rejection serves neither Palestinian interests nor the cause of peace.

I would go a step further. If, as I believe, the Clinton ideas embody the basic trade-offs that will be required in any peace deal, it is essential to understand them for what they were and not to misrepresent them. This is especially true now that the Bush administration, for the first time, seems to be contemplating a serious effort to deal with the core issues of the conflict.

Of course, one might ask if trying to address the core issues is appropriate at a moment when Palestinians are locked in an internal stalemate and the Israeli public lacks confidence in its government. Can politically weak leaders make compromises on the issues that go to the heart of the conflict? Can the Palestinian president, Mahmoud Abbas, compromise on the right of return and tell his public that refugees will not go back to Israel? Can Israel's prime minister, Ehud Olmert, tell his public that demography and practicality mean that the Arab neighborhoods of East Jerusalem will have Palestinian and not Israeli sovereignty?

The basic trade-offs require meeting Israeli needs on security and refugees on the one hand and Palestinian needs on territory and a capital in Arab East Jerusalem on the other. But producing such trade-offs won't simply come from calling for them. Instead, an environment must be created in which each side believes the other can act on peace and is willing to condition its public for the difficult compromises that will be necessary.

So long as mythologies can't be cast aside, and so long as the trade-offs on the core issues can't be embraced by Israelis or Palestinians, peace will remain forever on the horizon. If history tells us anything, it is that for peace-making to work, it must proceed on the basis of fact, not fiction.

Dennis Ross, envoy to the Middle East in the Clinton administration, is counselor of the Washington Institute for Near East Policy.

Chapter 2

Carter Center Defections

The Carter Center in Atlanta

Carter Center Defections

In the wake of the release of *Palestine: Peace Not Apartheid,* early critics included those affiliated with the Carter Center and Emory University. Professor Kenneth W. Stein, the William E. Schatten professor of contemporary Middle Eastern history, political science, and Israel studies at Emory and the director of the university's Institute for the Study of Modern Israel, was the first of this group to disassociate himself from Carter's book. Stein, Carter's adviser on Middle Eastern affairs for many years and the first executive director of the Emory-affiliated human rights center founded by the president, has been a Carter Center fellow on Middle East affairs since 1983.

In an early December 2006 resignation letter to Carter, Emory President Jim Wagner and Carter Center Executive Director John Hardman, Stein ended his 23-year association with the center. Stein, who had collaborated with Carter on an earlier book, *The Blood of Abraham,* charged that the president's newest work is "replete with factual errors, copied materials not cited, superficialities, glaring omissions, and simply invented segments." Stein detailed many of these flaws in his spring 2007 *Middle East Quarterly* essay, "My Problem With Jimmy Carter's Book."

Shortly after Stein submitted his letter, Melvin Konnor, a professor of anthropology at Emory, also disassociated himself from the Carter Center. In a letter to John Hardman, he declined a position on the center's advisory panel, and urged the center to distance itself from the former president's "irrevocably tarnished legacy." In his letter, Konnor objected to a passage in Carter's book which he said condoned terrorism. Speaking later at Brandeis University on Jan. 23, 2007, Carter apologized for that passage.

The Carter Center suffered yet more embarassment when 15 members of the advisory board resigned after concluding that Carter had turned to "malicious advocacy" for the Palestinians and against Israel. At a March 7, 2007 lecture, a George Washington University student mentioned the mass resignations and criticism from other sources, and asked the former president whether he would have written the book differently were he to do it again. To which Carter responded, "the book is necessary. It's absolutely accurate. No one has found any error of any substance in the book."

Carter then went on to diminish the role of the advisory board members, and concluded: "They all happen to be Jewish Americans. I understand the tremendous pressures on them, and their motivations, as well. And I have offered in every one of my letters to them my availability to come to their synagogue or any other forum where they would like me to appear to answer questions and to explain the purposes of my book."

Professor Kenneth Stein's December 2006 letter of resignation, ending his 23-year association with the Carter Center:

This note is to inform you that yesterday, I sent letters to President Jimmy Carter, Emory University President Jim Wagner, and Dr. John Hardman, Executive Director of the Carter Center resigning my position, effectively immediately, as Middle East Fellow of the Carter Center of Emory University. This ends my 23 year association with an institution that in some small way I helped shape and develop. My joint academic position in Emory College in the History and Political Science Departments, and, as Director of the Emory Institute for the Study of Modern Israel remains unchanged.

Many still believe that I have an active association with the Center and act as an adviser to President Carter; neither is the case. President Carter has intermittently continued to come to the Arab-Israeli Conflict class I teach in Emory College. He gives undergraduate students a fine first hand recollection of the Begin-Sadat negotiations of the late 1970s. Since I left the Center physically thirteen years ago, the Middle East program of the Center has waned as has my status as a Carter Center Fellow. For the record, I had nothing to do with the research, preparation, writing, or review of President Carter's recent publication. Any material which he used from the book we did together in 1984, *The Blood of Abraham,* he used unilaterally.

President Carter's book on the Middle East, a title too inflammatory to even print, is not based on unvarnished analyses; it is replete with factual errors, copied materials not cited, superficialities, glaring omissions, and simply invented segments. Aside from the one-sided nature of the book, meant to provoke, there are recollections cited from meetings where I was the third person in the room, and my notes of those meetings show little similarity to points claimed in the book. Being a former President does not give one a unique privilege to invent information or to unpack it with cuts, deftly slanted to provide a particular outlook. Having little access to Arabic and Hebrew sources, I believe, clearly handicapped his understanding and analyses of how history has unfolded over the last decade. Falsehoods, if repeated often enough become meta-truths, and they then can become the erroneous baseline for shaping and reinforcing attitudes and for policy-making. The history and interpreta-

Professor Kenneth Stein, once executive director of the Carter Center, resigned all affiliation with the center.

"[The book] is replete with factual errors, copied materials not cited, superficialities, glaring omissions, and simply invented segments."

"Aside from the one-sided nature of the book, meant to provoke, there are recollections cited from meetings where I was the third person in the room, and my notes of those meetings show little similarity to points claimed in the book."

tion of the Arab-Israeli conflict is already drowning in half-truths, suppositions, and self-serving myths; more are not necessary. In due course, I shall detail these points and reflect on their origins.

The decade I spent at the Carter Center (1983-1993) as the first permanent Executive Director and as the first Fellow were intellectually enriching for Emory as an institution, the general public, the interns who learned with us, and for me professionally. Setting standards for rigorous interchange and careful analyses spilled out to the other programs that shaped the Center's early years. There was mutual respect for all views; we carefully avoided polemics or special pleading. This book does not hold to those standards. My continued association with the Center leaves the impression that I am sanctioning a series of egregious errors and polemical conclusions which appeared in President Carter's book. I can not allow that impression to stand.

Through Emory College, I have continued my professional commitment to inform students and the general public about the history and politics of Israel, the Middle East, and American policies toward the region. I have tried to remain true to a life-time devotion to scholarly excellence based upon unvarnished analyses and intellectual integrity. I hold fast to the notion that academic settings and those in positions of influence must teach and not preach. Through Emory College, in public lectures, and in OPED writings, I have adhered to the strong belief that history must presented in context, and understood the way it was, not the way we wish it to be.

"Having little access to Arabic and Hebrew sources, I believe, clearly handicapped his understanding and analyses of how history was unfolded over the last decade."

In closing, let me thank you for your friendship, past and continuing support for ISMI, and to Emory College. Let me also wish you and your loved ones a happy holiday season, and a healthy and productive new year.

As ever,
Ken
Dr. Kenneth W. Stein,
Professor of Contemporary Middle Eastern History,
Political Science, and Israeli Studies
Director, Middle East Research Program and
Emory Institute for the Study of Modern Israel, Atlanta, Georgia

Middle East Quarterly
Spring 2007

My Problem with Jimmy Carter's Book

by Kenneth W. Stein

Jimmy Carter's engagement in foreign affairs as a former president is unprecedented in U.S. history. Because he regards the Arab-Israeli conflict as among Washington's most important foreign policy topics, he has written more than two dozen articles and commentaries about the conflict, eight in the past year alone. In these publications, Carter uses his credibility as a former president, Nobel laureate, and key player in the September 1978 Camp David accords and the Egypt-Israel peace treaty to unfold his set of truths and often to criticize U.S. policy. He relishes the role of elder statesman and believes that with his accrued wisdom and experience, he can contribute to solutions.

But *Palestine: Peace Not Apartheid,*[1] Carter's twenty-first book and his second to focus on the Arab-Israeli conflict, is deficient. He does what no non-fiction author should ever do: He allows ideology or opinion to get in the way of facts. While Carter says that he wrote the book to educate and provoke debate, the narrative aims its attack toward Israel, Israeli politicians, and Israel's supporters. It contains egregious errors of both commission and omission. To suit his desired ends, he manipulates information, redefines facts, and exaggerates conclusions. Falsehoods, when repeated and backed by the prestige of Carter's credentials, can comprise an erroneous baseline for shaping and reinforcing attitudes and policymaking. Rather than bring peace, they can further fuel hostilities, encourage retrenchment, and hamper peacemaking.

"Remember Ken, Only One of Us Was President"

I first met Carter at a 1982 reception welcoming him to Emory University. He invited me to serve as the Carter Center's first permanent executive director, a position I held between 1983 and 1986, and as the center's Middle East fellow, an association I continued until December 2006 when I resigned that post over both the inaccuracies in *Palestine: Peace Not Apartheid* and its message, which contradicts the Carter Center's founding purposes.

My tasks as Middle East fellow included writing memoranda for Carter about Middle Eastern issues, taking notes at virtually all Carter meetings that addressed Middle Eastern issues, preparing a monthly analysis of events, coordinating major Middle East conferences, and planning Middle Eastern trips. I accompanied Carter as a political adviser and press liaison on three lengthy Middle Eastern trips in March 1983, March 1987, and March 1990.

Jimmy Carter "had little patience for precedent or laborious recapitulation of history," said Stein, who co-authored *The Blood of Abraham* with Carter. In the book, the ex-president erroneously charges that Menachem Begin "wanted to expand Israeli borders to both sides of the Jordan River"

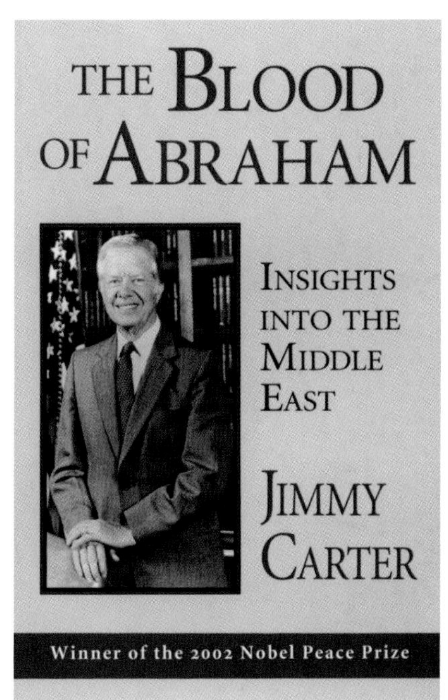

As we collaborated on *The Blood of Abraham,*[2] Carter's first book about the Middle East, I witnessed Carter's passion, determination, and stubbornness. He was capable of absorbing vast amounts of information, and he had an extraordinary capacity to recall detailed points and concepts almost verbatim months after reading them.

Carter's preferred method in writing the book was to lay a brief and somewhat selective historical foundation for each chapter and emphasize the contemporary. I sought to anchor each chapter more deeply in history and political culture. He had little patience for precedent or laborious recapitulation of history. Too often it interfered with his desire to find action-oriented solutions, which befit his training as an engineer. For Carter, history and ideology bestowed unwanted moorings and unnecessary rigidities; they shackled the pragmatism and flexibility of the would-be negotiator.

Our relationship was honest. We established a mutual respect and capacity to criticize each other. He asked me not to hold back. I often pressed him on balance, especially when, throughout the 1980s, he criticized the Israeli government repeatedly for obstructing renewed negotiations. While writing *The Blood of Abraham,* we argued over word choice, phrases, and claims. Once, when I disagreed too strenuously, Carter impishly smiled and, with his blue-eyes twinkling, said, "Remember, Ken, only one of us was president of the United States." Still, he always listened.

While Carter is a regular guest lecturer in my classes, I last sat down with him for a substantive talk in June 2002. At that meeting, I showed Carter a map of Israeli settlements in the West Bank and Gaza, emphasized the protective aspect of the separation fence that was then being constructed, and suggested that the ensuing division might contribute to the achievement of a two-state solution, something we both sought. Carter viewed the fence as proof that the Israeli government sought to wall in the Palestinians. Several days after our meeting, he wrote an op-ed condemning the U.S. government's alignment with Israel and Washington's unwillingness to pursue talks with Palestinian leaders.[3] His commentary came against the backdrop of White House demands to make engagement conditional upon a Palestinian cessation of terrorism.[4]

The Roots of Carter's Anger

Carter's grievance list against Israel is long: He believes the Israeli government's failure to withdraw fully from the West Bank is illegal and immoral; he condemns settlement construction; and he lambastes its current human rights abuse in the West Bank, which he labels "one of the worst examples of human rights abuse I know."[5] From the time he was president, he has criticized Israel's confiscation of Palestinian land, usurpation of water rights, and retaliatory bulldozing of Palestinian houses. Such policies, he has argued, are responsible for the moribund Palestinian economy. Carter holds particular animus toward the security barrier, first proposed by the late prime minister and Nobel Peace Prize winner Yitzhak Rabin,[6] as the latest example of what he believes to be a policy of de facto annexation of the West Bank.

Carter sees the Israeli-Palestinian conflict as the root of both U.S. unpopularity in the region and the wider problem of Middle East instability. Once the historic injustice done to the Palestinians is resolved, he believes, other issues plaguing U.S. foreign policy will dissipate, if not disappear.

Carter believes the conflict's resolution to be simple: After the Israeli government agrees in principle to withdraw fully from the West Bank, a dedicated negotiator like himself can usher in an independent, peaceful Palestinian state. That this has not happened is, in Carter's view, primarily due to the legacy of late Israeli prime minister Menachem Begin, not the fault of poor Palestinian decision-making or the Palestinian embrace of terrorism. The intransigence of Begin and his successors, Carter believes, was compounded by a failure of U.S. political leaders to pressure the Israeli government to correct its policy. Washington's failure to lead, he believes, is heavily due to the failure of American supporters of Israel to criticize the Jewish state.

Carter believes that if the U.S. government reduces or stops its support for Israel, then the Jewish state will be weakened and become more malleable in negotiations. His underlying logic is based upon an imperial rationality that assumes Washington to have the answer to myriad issues besetting Middle Eastern societies. This plays into the notion in Arab societies that the cause of their problems lies with Western powers and other outsiders. *Palestine: Peace Not Apartheid* will feed that belief.

In the book, Carter does not mention the counterproductive judgments made by Palestinian leaders or their embrace of terrorism over the last many years. While nineteenth- and twentieth-century European, Ottoman, Arab, and Zionist leaders all sought at various times to stifle Palestinian self-determination, the claim that the establishment of a Palestinian state rests only in the hands of Jerusalem and Washington is rubbish. By adopting so completely the Palestinian historical narrative, Carter may hamper diplomatic efforts enshrined in the "Road Map" and elsewhere that attempt to compel the Palestinian leadership to accept accountability for its actions. In pursuing this path, Carter violates the advice he gave eighty Palestinian business, religious, and political leaders on March 16, 1983, when, speaking to a gathering at the U.S. consulate in

"Carter's feelings on Israel were always ambivalent. On the one hand, he felt Israel was being intransigent; on the other, he genuinely had an attachment to the country as the 'land of the Bible,'"

—former National Security Advisor Zbigniew Brzezinski

Jerusalem, he said, "Unless you take your own destiny into your own hands and stop relying on others," you will not have a state.[7]

Carter's distrust of the U.S. Jewish community and other supporters of Israel runs deep. According to former national security advisor Zbigniew Brzezinski, "Carter's feelings on Israel were always ambivalent. On the one hand, he felt Israel was being intransigent; on the other, he genuinely had an attachment to the country as the 'land of the Bible.'"[8]

In a 1991 research interview with Carter for my book *Heroic Diplomacy: Sadat, Kissinger, Carter, Begin and the Quest for Arab-Israeli Peace,*[9] Carter recollected that:

> [Vice president] Fritz Mondale was much more deeply immersed in the Jewish organization leadership than I was. That was an alien world to me. They [American Jews] didn't support me during the presidential campaign [that] had been predicated greatly upon Jewish money ... Almost all of them were supportive of Scoop Jackson—Scoop Jackson was their spokesman ... their hero. So I was looked upon as an alien challenger to their own candidate. You know, I don't mean unanimously but ... overwhelmingly. So I didn't feel obligated to them or to labor unions and so forth. Fritz ... was committed to Israel ... It was an act just like breathing to him—it wasn't like breathing to me. So I was willing to break the shell more than he was.[10]

"Mondale was much more deeply immersed in the Jewish organization leadership than I was. That was an alien world to me. They [American Jews] didn't support me during the presidential campaign [that] had been predicated greatly upon Jewish money ..."

—Jimmy Carter

Jimmy Carter campaigns with Walter Mondale in 1980

The gap between many American Jews and Carter grew during his presidency as Carter increased pressure on Jerusalem. In the 1980 general election, Carter received a lower proportion of Jewish votes than any Democratic presidential candidate since 1920.

The Ghost of Menachem Begin

Carter's animosity toward Begin has grown with time. He blames Begin for refusing to negotiate over the West Bank. Not only did this deny Carter a more complete peace deal, but, Carter believes, it also institutionalized itself in Israeli policymaking, worsening the Palestinians' plight. Since Begin took office on May 17, 1977, ending the Labor movement's hegemony in Israeli political life, Carter has repeatedly blasted Israeli prime ministers for what he terms the creation of a "horrible" and "terrible" state of affairs for the Palestinians in areas of east Jerusalem, the West Bank, and the Gaza Strip.

The mistrust was mutual and began to surface before Begin's election. According to Eliyahu Ben-Elissar, then Begin's bureau chief, "Begin did not like [Carter's] March 1977 statement that the Palestinian refugees needed a homeland. None of us liked it. We resented it ... Begin considered it a major shift in U.S. policy."[11]

Indeed, skepticism of Carter's intentions may have convinced Begin to take a harder line about the West Bank, which, in line with biblical terminology, he called Judea and Samaria. During his tenure as prime minister, Begin forbade the negotiation agenda to include the West Bank and those portions of Jerusalem that the Israeli government annexed after the 1967 Six-Day war. This refusal to negotiate became Carter's core disagreement with Begin. Carter realized that with Begin adamant against further concessions, he had no tangible item to offer to the Palestinians or other Arab leaders to reach a broader peace agreement. With Begin not offering a fallback position, Carter could not initiate a conclusive Israeli-Palestinian negotiating process. He never forgave Begin.

Intertwined in the dispute over the West Bank was the issue of Israeli settlements. Samuel Lewis, U.S. ambassador to Israel at the time, explained, "Begin would never consider admitting that the [Israeli] right to settle wasn't a right, and Carter, basically, was asking him [Begin] to agree that settlements were illegal."[12] Begin refused. The subsequent expansion of settlements has further embittered Carter's relations with Israeli leaders and with Israel's supporters in the United States, whom he believes are willfully silent on the subject.

While Carter lauds Begin for his intelligence, a point he has repeatedly made when speaking to my students, his animus toward the late Israeli leader is limitless. This became evident when we were writing *The Blood of Abraham,* and Carter insisted on asserting that Begin "wanted to expand Israeli borders to both sides of the Jordan River." In fact, this is anachronistic. True, this had been Begin's view prior to Israel's independence in 1948, but it was not, as Carter implied, Begin's position after his twenty-nine years in the Knesset (parliament) or during his premiership. During chapter editing, I brought the error to Carter's attention. He declined to correct it.[13]

"During difficult negotiations between Egypt and Israel, Carter and his team tried to get Sadat to engage in a collusive scheme ... Thus, Carter risked possible Israel-Egyptian peace in an effort to extract greater concessions from Begin."

Begin (left) with Carter and Sadat at Camp David in 1978

During the difficult negotiations between Egypt and Israel, Carter and his advisers tried to get Sadat to engage in a collusive scheme: They would encourage Sadat to make "deliberately exaggerated" demands. The White House would then intervene to "compel" Cairo to scale back its demands in exchange for Israeli concessions. Then-national security advisor Brzezinski explained that Washington would "apply maximum leverage on Israel to accommodate,"[14] by keeping the West Bank's political future on the table for future negotiations. That Carter risked possible Israeli-Egyptian peace in an effort to extract greater concessions from Begin underscores the tension in their relationship.

In 1983, the first time Begin met Carter after both had left office, Begin was icy toward the ex-president. Carter surmised that he may have "aggravated him [Begin] more than usual."[15] Begin's personal secretary later said Begin was angry with what he had learned in the books by Brzezinski and National Security Council staff member William B. Quandt about Carter's behind-the-scenes maneuvering. This anger grew after he read the claim in *The Blood of Abraham* regarding his alleged desire to expand Israeli borders across the Jordan River.[16] On our 1987 trip to Israel, Begin refused to see Carter, citing health reasons, but Begin's personal secretary told me it was because of the way Carter had treated Begin.

Carter also blames difficulties with Begin for undermining his re-election. In early 1980, with the critical New York Democratic primary looming, Mondale urged Carter to repudiate the U.S. vote for U.N. Security Council Resolution (UNSCR) 465,[17] which had condemned Israeli settlement activity. According to Brzezinski:

> Jewish voters swung heavily over to Senator [Edward] Kennedy, ensuring Carter's defeat. The set-back prolonged the Carter-Kennedy contest. Sadat did

> not want a final showdown on the Palestinian problem prior to the return of the Sinai to Egypt. Without pressure from Sadat, our own incentive to push Israel hard was much decreased. Begin proved himself to be a skilled manipulator ... adroit at delaying tactics and in diversionary public appeals ... by mid-June it was clear even to Mondale that Begin wanted Carter defeated.[18]

According to Brzezinski, Carter believed his disagreement with Begin to have both cost him critical primary victories and to have weakened his re-election bid.[19] But other issues—high inflation and mortgage rates, the Iran hostage crisis, a national sense of malaise, and the third party candidature of John Anderson—may have contributed more to Carter's loss.

Conflating Flexibility and Fact

Carter possesses missionary zeal. He believes that had he won re-election, he would have succeeded in ending the Israeli-Palestinian conflict. Numerous times during the 1980s, Carter quipped after leaving meetings with Middle Eastern or U.S. officials that, if given a chance, he could "make this happen." In order to convey a sense that Middle Eastern leaders or Washington officials trusted him and wanted him to continue to mediate, he would open remarks to either of them with, "I was authorized to report ...."

Carter has come to scorn those who disagree with him. On his recent book tour promoting *Palestine: Peace Not Apartheid,* whenever an interviewer disagreed with a premise or challenged Carter's views, he would respond, "It is obvious you did not read my book." This is Carter's way of chiding the interviewer for not accepting his wisdom. When Carter says, "Everything in the book is accurate; it is correct," he seeks acknowledgment that he possesses a privileged understanding of the conflict's fundamental truths and should, therefore, be accepted as someone qualified to apportion blame. In his 2005 book, *Our Endangered Values: America's Moral Crisis,*[20] Carter speaks from a similar peremptory pulpit.[21]

But Carter is often wrong. Throughout *Palestine: Peace Not Apartheid,* he allows his premises to supplant the facts. His book contains no footnotes, citations, or sources. It contains an appendix and a series of maps, some of which he seems to have mislabeled and taken from Clinton-era negotiator Dennis Ross' *The Missing Peace: The Inside Story of the Fight for Middle East Peace.*[22] The maps are reconfigured to support Carter's statement that Israel's best offer in the final months of Clinton's presidency was to divide the West Bank into three non-contiguous areas, thus reinforcing Carter's claim of apartheid.[23] Carter dismissed the allegation that he appropriated the maps, saying that he had never seen Ross's book.[24] If true, Carter ignored the most important and detailed memoir yet published on 1990s-era Arab-Israeli negotiations.

Carter has come to scorn those who disagree with him. On his recent book tour promoting *Palestine: Peace Not Apartheid,* whenever an interviewer disagreed with a premise or challenged Carter's views, he would respond, "It is obvious you did not read my book."

In the book, Carter often uses selective remarks by others to advocate his preferences. He uses the literary device "many believe" or "many say" to avoid tying a statement to himself. While implying that the Israeli government practices apartheid vis-à-vis the Palestinians, Carter refrains from calling Israelis racist but highlights and leaves unanswered the late Syrian president Hafez al-Assad's opinion:

> Assad asserted that the Jews of the world constitute one people, regardless of obvious differences in their identities, languages, customs, and citizenship, but deny that the Palestinians comprise a coherent people even though they have one national identity, one language, one culture, and one history. Many Arabs consider these distinctions to be a form of racism by which Israelis regard Palestinian Arabs as inferiors who are not worthy of basic human rights, often branding them as terrorists if they resist Israel's encroachments.[25]

Nowhere in *The Blood of Abraham* did Carter cite such an account of Assad's views. Perhaps Carter had an additional communication with Assad, but the notes I have of our three extensive meetings with Assad in 1983, 1987, and 1990 do not support such statements. Regardless, his new emphasis of Assad's views segues with publication of *Palestine: Peace Not Apartheid,* "that Israelis regard Palestinian Arabs as inferiors." If Carter wanted to tar Israel as racist, this was a clever way of doing it.

Carter is frustrated with his successors' Middle East policies. He believes they did not share the concern (George W. Bush), intellectual competence (Ronald Reagan), determination (George H.W. Bush), or experience necessary to pull off a negotiated solution. He believes Bill Clinton could have done a better job at the 2000 Camp David summit between Palestinian Liberation Organization (PLO) chairman Yasir Arafat and Israeli prime minister Ehud Barak.

Conversely, Carter is convinced that he himself was the essential ingredient to enable the Egyptian-Israeli peace.[26] However, Carter does not understand how fortunate he was to have in Begin and Sadat two leaders who needed agreement. Each possessed vision and courage and faced a common adversary in the Soviet Union. This reality welded them into uncomfortable but necessary interaction. Had Carter continued his diplomacy into a second term, he would not have found Israeli and Palestinian leaders possessing any degree of urgency for a solution. There is no evidence that the Arafat of the early 1980s was more willing to compromise or abandon terror than the Arafat faced by Clinton. Nonetheless, Carter believes his negotiating skills could bear fruit where Clinton failed. His conviction is so great that he need not read Ross's account.

Errors of Revision

A survey of Carter's speeches and writings over the last quarter century reveals the evolution of his views. He has shifted from annoyance to exasperation, from frustration to anger, and from partial blame upon the Palestinians to their exculpation. In recent years, though, he has moved even further, using invented facts to support his desired conclusion.

Evidence of his slide from would-be mediator to unabashed advocate for the Palestinians appears in his partisan rendition of four U.N. resolutions: U.N. Security Council Resolution 465 (1980); U.N. General Assembly Resolution 194 (1948); U.N. Security Council Resolution 242 (1967); and U.N. Security

Council Resolution 338 (1973). *Palestine: Peace Not Apartheid* is the first Carter book to emphasize UNSCR 465, in which the U.N.:

> Determines that all measures taken by Israel to change the physical character, demographic composition, institutional structure or status of the Palestinian and other Arab territories occupied since 1967, including Jerusalem, or any part thereof, have no legal validity and that Israel's policy and practices of settling parts of its population and new immigrants in those territories constitute a flagrant violation of the Fourth Geneva Convention.

Carter's use of UNSCR 465 is an example of how he uses accurate information but omits part of the story to bolster his presentation. He wants to show Israel to be in violation of international law by being present in the territories. While he cites the unanimous passage of UNSCR 465 to suggest that there was universal condemnation of Israel's position with regard to east Jerusalem,[27] he omits that two days after its passage, he himself disavowed the U.S. assent to the resolution. At the time, he said the resolution was a mistake which resulted from a "failure to communicate" between the State Department and Donald F. McHenry, the U.S. ambassador to the United Nations.[28]

Carter also omits the possibility that the vote may have certified for Begin his conviction that Carter could not be trusted. Just two hours before the vote, Secretary of State Cyrus Vance had assured the Israeli ambassador, Ephraim Evron, that all references to Jerusalem would be removed.[29]

Carter is also less than complete in his discussion of U.N. General Assembly Resolution 194. Many Palestinians cite the resolution as an unequivocal endorsement by the international community of the right of Palestinian refugees to return to their homes in present-day Israel or be compensated if they choose not to exercise that right.[30] Carter accepts this view and implies its universality. He does not acknowledge the fact that five Arab states—Egypt, Iraq, Lebanon, Saudi Arabia, and Syria—voted against the resolution in protest of its implied recognition of Israel.

Two hours before the 1980 UN Security Council vote on Resolution 465, Carter's Secretary of State, Cyrus Vance, falsely assured the Israelis that the resolution would not refer to Jerusalem.

Having rarely mentioned this resolution—which has never been a part of U.S.-brokered peace agreements in the region—until the publication of his most recent book, Carter's endorsement of the Palestinian interpretation of Resolution 194 appears more motivated by a desire to position himself as a trusted negotiator for the Arab side than by epistemology.[31] However, in legitimizing a maximalist reading of Resolution 194, Carter flirts with the de-legitimization of Israel as a Jewish state. Hence, within *Palestine: Peace Not Apartheid,* Carter is inconsistent about the right of return, at times suggesting it would apply only to the West Bank, Gaza, and East Jerusalem[32] while elsewhere suggesting the right of return would enable Palestinians to return to Israel proper.[33] On his book tour, Carter sidestepped the issue by endorsing the implementation of "all relevant U.N. resolutions."

Whereas Carter had earlier written that "Israel would decide unilaterally how many Palestinians" would be admitted to Israel "or could return to Palestine or receive appropriate compensation as a fulfillment of UN Security Resolution 194,"[34] his use of the indefinite article "a" in front of "fulfillment" suggests he may harbor multiple interpretations of Palestinian refugee settlement.

Palestinians are less flexible. By demanding Israeli adherence to Resolution 194, Carter ignores the Arabic-language writings of Palestinian officials who say that the Palestinian leadership will never give up the right of return to what is now Israel. In response to Clinton's proposals to allow Palestinian refugees the right to return only to a Palestinian state in the West Bank and Gaza, the Palestinian Authority declared:

> Resolution 194, which is the basis for a just settlement of the refugee problem, determines the return of the Palestinian refugees "to their homes" and not "to their homeland" or "to historical Palestine." The essence of the right of return is freedom of choice: The Palestinians must be given the right to choose where they live, and that includes returning to the homes out of which they were driven.[35]

Carter, however, scrubs clean Palestinian intransigence.

UNSCR 242 and 338 remain the resolutions around which diplomats center efforts to negotiate a settlement. In its preamble, UNSCR 242 notes "the inadmissibility of the acquisition of territory by war" and, in its operative portion, calls for "withdrawal of Israeli armed forces from territories occupied in the recent conflict." Nowhere in the resolution does it stipulate what or where Israel's borders should be, nor does the resolution mandate Israeli withdrawal from all territories taken in the 1967 war. This is not a parsing of an arbitrary phrase; it took five months to negotiate and endorse the intentional ambiguity embodied in the language of the resolution.[36] Carter revises UNSCR 242, though, saying it "confirmed Israel's existence within its 1949 borders as promised in the Camp David Accords and Oslo Agreement" and that it states "Israel must withdraw from occupied territories."[37] Later, he writes that UNSCR 242 "mandates" and "requires" Israeli withdrawal.[38]

This reinterpretation is invention on Carter's part. He first adopted this revision of UNSCR 242 in his December 10, 2002 Nobel Peace Prize acceptance speech when he referred to "withdrawal from the occupied territories." Speaking at the Council on Foreign Relations on March 2, 2006, he used a similar phrase and added the false claim that Begin had agreed to Carter's reinterpretation of UNSCR 242 at Camp David in 1978.[39] In effect, Carter is changing the "Land for Peace" formula into "Land for Negotiations." The idea that negotiations should only occur subsequent to Israeli withdrawal was the position held by the PLO at the height of its terrorist campaign in the 1970s.

UNSCR 338 receives similar treatment. Carter alters its call for "negotiations between the parties"—a formulation that would require recognition of Israel—into a call for international mediation, a position that would embolden continued Hamas and Islamic Jihad rejectionism.

Excusing Terrorism

Among the most troubling aspects of *Palestine: Peace Not Apartheid* is Carter's apparent willingness to condone the killing of Israelis. He is deliberate with words. When he writes, "It is imperative that the general Arab community and all significant Palestinian groups make it clear that they will end the suicide bombings and other acts of terrorism *when* international laws and the ultimate goals of the Roadmap for Peace are accepted by Israel,"[40] he leaves the impression that it is legitimate to engage in terrorism and suicide bombing against Israelis until Jerusalem accepts his interpretation of international law. In doing so, he ignores the fact that the performance-based formula for advancing Israeli-Palestinian talks, the so-called "Road Map" endorsed by the Quartet in 2003, required immediate cessation of terrorism.

To support *Palestine: Peace Not Apartheid's* central theme that Israel is intransigent, Carter recasts Hamas as a moderate partner ready to negotiate with Israel. He launders its reputation both with careful word choice and omission. He uses the past tense, for example, to describe Hamas as an "Islamic militant group that *opposed* recognition of Israel [and] *perpetrated* acts of violence." Carter adds that he "urged them ...to forgo violence."[41] He omits mention that Hamas denies the right of a Jewish state to exist in the Middle East and the group's belief that historical Palestine belongs in its entirety to Muslims. Carter is incorrect when he writes that Hamas has not been responsible for any terrorist acts since August 2004.[42] Hamas on many subsequent occasions claimed responsibility for firing Qassam rockets into Israel and also claimed responsibility for the kidnapping of Gilad Shalit in June 2006.[43]

Carter also claims that Hamas supports a 2002 Arab summit resolution which advocates a two-state solution, albeit one dependent on the right of return of Palestinian refugees. But Hamas rejects the two-state solution. Carter states that Ismail Haniyeh, the Hamas leader in the West Bank and Gaza Strip, "supports peace talks between Israel and [Palestinian Authority leader] Abbas ... [and] accepts the Road Map in its entirety." He does not. Carter adds that Hamas would modify its rejection of Israel if there were a negotiated agreement that the Palestinian people can approve, "an important facet of the Camp David Accords,"[44] but the Camp David accords never specified universal Palestinian ratification.

Carter has defended Hamas against charges of intransigence during his *Palestine: Peace Not Apartheid* book tour. While visiting Tehran on December 8, 2006, Haniyeh said, "We will never recognize the usurper Zionist government and will continue our jihadist movement until Bayt al-Maqdis [Jerusalem] and the Al-Aqsa Mosque are liberated."[45] When asked by a Denver radio host on station KHOW 630 AM six days later about Haniyeh's statement, Carter answered, "No, he didn't. No, he did not do that. I did not hear that."

Carter's resistance to contrary evidence contrasts with the impatience some Palestinians and intellectuals have for Hamas's rejectionism. On June 4, 2006, for example, Palestinian analyst Muhammad Yaghi wrote:

> The problem with Hamas' political platform is its rejection of the principle of the two states on the historical land of Palestine ... This position cannot be accepted internationally, and certainly Israel cannot accept it. On the contrary, this position gives the international community the justifications to turn its back to us and gives Israel enough pretexts to refuse withdrawal and continue its attacks and unilateral solutions. Hamas' political platform is political suicide and cannot constitute the basis for any political agreement.[46]

Inventing History

After reading *Palestine: Peace Not Apartheid,* I was troubled by a passage recounting a meeting Carter and I had attended with Assad at his presidential office in March 1990. I revisited my notes and saw discrepancies between them and the story Carter recounts. When discussing the Syrian dispute with Israel, Assad, as always, chose his words carefully. The notes show the following passage:

> **JC:** Your severest critics know you keep your word—would you accept demilitarization of [the] Golan Heights?
>
> **A:** Today, Peres [Israel's foreign minister] said Syria would accept [a] demilitarized Golan. But we cannot accept this because we are sacrificing our sovereignty.
>
> **A:** In the past we have said that things must be done mutually on both sides of the Golan—international forces, semi-demilitarization—on equal footing. If anyone can ask for additional measures, we should ask for a larger DMZ [demilitarized zone] from their part.

But, in *Palestine: Peace Not Apartheid,* Carter wrote:

> When I visited Damascus in 1990, President Assad informed me that he was willing to negotiate with Israel on the status of the Golan Heights. His proposal was that both sides withdraw from the international border, with a small force of foreign observers and electronic devices to monitor the neutral zone. When I asked him if each nation would have to fall back an equal distance, he replied that Syria might move its troops farther from the border because of the terrain. He also gave me permission to report his proposal to Washington and to the Israelis, which I did in Jerusalem three days later.[47]

Carter reworded the conversation to suggest that Assad was flexible and the Israelis were not. Assad did not say he would accept a demilitarized zone; to do so would be to sacrifice his sovereignty. Nor did he say he would withdraw deeper from his side of the border. This was not a slip of memory for Carter; Carter received a full set of my notes of the March 1990 trip after its conclusion. These were intentional distortions.

When the meeting with Assad ended, Carter held a press conference at the Sheraton Damascus Hotel. In response to a journalist's question about the substance of a possible Syrian-Israeli agreement to include the future of the Golan Heights, Carter said, "I don't think you could expect the Syrians to demilitarize five kilometers on their borders without an equal demilitarization on the Israeli side of the border. But with an equivalent, negotiated, mutual establishment of a demilitarized zone, I think there it would be feasible, yes. I don't think that you can expect one side to demilitarize an area and not have an equivalent demilitarization on the other side of the border. This is something that is a matter of national pride, of national prestige. But I don't think there is any alternative to what I have just proposed. Let me say again, I am not speaking for anyone except myself."[48]

"What Carter stated as his personal opinion in the 1990 press conference, he transmits as fact in 2006 in his book. He puts words in Assad's mouth."

What Carter stated as his personal opinion in the 1990 press conference, he transmits as fact in 2006 in his book. He puts words in Assad's mouth. Carter invented the substance of this meeting to indicate that Assad was leaning toward flexibility. Assad only considered demilitarized zones in his negotiations with the Israelis after the Soviet Union's collapse removed his greatest patron. Assad certainly did not say that Syria would withdraw deeper from his side of the border. These are intentional changes that Carter made for the apparent purpose of misrepresenting Israeli intransigence and Arab state flexibility.

Conclusions

Timing is everything. Had Carter always viewed the issue of settlements with the severity he does now, he might have told Begin privately, if not publicly, that aid to Israel would be conditioned upon the cessation of their construction. At the time there were fewer than 20,000 settlers in the West Bank. However unpopular such a policy would have been, Carter would have not caved in either to Israeli leaders or U.S. supporters of Israel. Carter believes or asserts he had won a five-year, rather than three-month, commitment from Begin not to build settlements, but there is no doubt that Begin only committed himself to three months.[49] In Sadat's eyes, Carter looked foolish because of Begin's build-up of settlements. By the time Sadat and Begin signed the Egypt-Israel peace treaty, Carter was focused on other foreign policy matters and how his policies toward the conflict would influence his support in upcoming primaries and the general election.

Had Carter won re-election, he might have recommitted himself to the task of reaching an Israeli-Palestinian agreement. It is a historical "what if?" In Carter's mind, he would have succeeded. Historians are less sure. Negotiating over Jerusalem's future and the West Bank would have been more complex, if not impossible, than the discussions over Sinai. Arafat was not Sadat, and many Arab states remained opposed to Israel's right to exist. The Islamic Revolution in Iran bolstered radicalism. As for Begin, he did not regard the forfeiture of the West Bank, let alone the annexed portions of Jerusalem, as negotiable issues. The obstacles to progress, then, were virtually insurmountable.

Carter is correct that settlements complicate negotiations. Disputes over expropriated land increase in proportion to their numbers. Here, his position is consistent with that of his successors. Carter is also correct that if there is to be any long-term solution to the Palestinian-Israeli conflict, there should be a two-state solution in which both Israel as a Jewish state and a Palestinian Arab state are independent on contiguous land and free from external intrusion. For this to happen, there must be courage, vision, leadership, and a willingness to abandon myths, fictions, and a cult of martyrdom.

Conflict resolution requires precision to supplant ambiguity. Both Israelis and Palestinians will have to abandon exclusive claim to all land west of the Jordan River. Israel's withdrawal from Gaza in August 2005, even if unilateral, was an important step. If the Palestinians are to have an independent state, they will have to forfeit support by radical states, abandon terrorism, and end their rejection of Israel.

The best option for peace is perhaps one that was offered thirty years ago when, on March 9, 1977, President Jimmy Carter said "recognized borders have to be mutual ... where sovereignty is mutually agreed. Defense lines may or may not conform to those legal borders. There may be extensions of Israeli defense beyond the permanent and recognized borders."[50] Unlike the narrative in *Palestine: Peace Not Apartheid,* Carter at that time was accurate, temperate, and practical.

Kenneth W. Stein is professor of contemporary Middle Eastern history and political science and director of the Institute for the Study of Modern Israel at Emory University. *He thanks Jonathan Schanzer, Bruce Maddy-Weitzman, and Eran Lehrman for their advice.*

1. New York: Simon & Schuster, 2006 (288 pp., $27).
2. Boston: Houghton Mifflin, 1985.
3. Jimmy Carter, "Mideast Needs a New Mediator," *USA Today,* July 1, 2002.
4. See, for example, "President Bush Calls for New Palestinian Leadership," Office of the Press Secretary, June 24, 2002.
5. Interview with Jimmy Carter, "Hardball with Chris Matthews," MSNBC, Nov. 28, 2006.
6. David Makovsky, "How to Build a Fence," *Foreign Affairs,* Mar./Apr. 2004, p. 52.
7. Author's notes on Jimmy Carter's meetings with Palestinian notables, American Consulate, east Jerusalem, Mar. 12, 1983.
8. Zbigniew Brzezinski, *Power and Principle: Memoirs of the National Security Adviser, 1977-1981* (New York: Farrar Straus Giroux, 1983), p. 83.
9. New York: Routledge, 1999.
10. Author interview with Jimmy Carter, Atlanta, Feb. 19, 1991.
11. Author interview with Eliyahu Ben-Elissar, Jerusalem, Nov. 13, 1992.
12. Remarks by Samuel Lewis, The United States Institute for Peace, minutes of a study group session on *Lessons Learned from Fifty Years of Negotiating Experiences,* Washington, D.C., Apr. 16, 1991.

13. Carter, *The Blood of Abraham,* p. 42.
14. Brzezinski, *Power and Principle,* pp. 242-7.
15. Carter, *The Blood of Abraham,* p. 107.
16. Author interview with Yahiel Kadishai, Begin's secretary (1977-83) and confidante, July 5, 1993, Tel Aviv.
17. UNSC Resolution 465: "Territories Occupied by Israel," Mar. 1, 1980.
18. Brzezinksi, *Power and Principle,* pp. 442-3.
19. Ibid.
20. New York: Simon & Schuster, 2005.
21. John Derbyshire, "Nasty Piece of Work: Our Endangered Values: America's Moral Crisis," *National Review,* Jan. 30, 2006.
22. New York: Farrar, Straus and Giroux, 2004.
23. Dennis Ross interview by Wolf Blitzer, "The Situation Room," CNN, Dec. 8, 2006; Dennis Ross, "Don't Play with Maps," *The New York Times,* Jan. 9, 2007.
24. Jimmy Carter interview, *Fox News, Special Report with Brit Hume,* Dec. 8, 2006.
25. Carter, *Palestine: Peace Not Apartheid,* p. 77.
26. Kenneth W. Stein, *Heroic Diplomacy: Sadat, Kissinger, Carter, Begin and the Quest for Arab-Israeli Peace* (New York: Routledge, 1999), pp. 40-1, 252-5.
27. Carter, Palestine: *Peace Not Apartheid,* p. 52.
28. Allan J. Mayer, "Newly Vulnerable Carter," Newsweek, Mar. 17, 1980.
29. Ibid.
30. Article XI states, "the refugees wishing to return to their homes and live at peace with their neighbours should be permitted to do so at the earliest practicable date, and that compensation should be paid for the property of those choosing not to return and for loss of or damage to property which, under principles of international law or in equity, should be made good by the Governments or authorities responsible."
31. For a similar statement of Carter's attitude toward issues and negotiations, see Peter G. Bourne, *Jimmy Carter* (New York: Scribner, 1997), p. 495.
32. Carter, *Palestine: Peace Not Apartheid,* p. 28.
33. Ibid., p. 167.
34. Carter, *The Blood of Abraham,* p. 168.
35. *Al-Ayyam* (Ramallah), Jan. 2, 2001.
36. The most detailed overview and analysis of UNSC Resolution 242's evolution may be found in *U.N. Security Council Resolution 242: The Building Block for Peacemaking* (Washington: Washington Institute for Near East Policy, 1993).
37. Carter, *Palestine: Peace Not Apartheid,* p. 38.
38. Ibid., pp. 207, 208.
39. "Peace versus Democracy in Palestine: A Conversation with Jimmy Carter," Council on Foreign Relations, Mar. 2, 2006.
40. Carter, *Palestine: Peace Not Apartheid,* p. 213. Emphasis added. Speaking at Brandeis University on Jan. 23, 2007, Carter acknowledged this sentence to be "worded in an absolutely improper and stupid way."
41. Ibid., p. 144.
42. Ibid., p. 184.
43. *The Washington Post,* June 27, 2006.
44. Carter, *Palestine: Peace Not Apartheid,* p. 186.
45. Voice of the Islamic Republic of Iran radio, Dec. 8, 2006, 07:50 GMT, in Persian, as transcribed by *BBC Worldwide Monitoring.*
46. *Al-Ayyam,* June 4, 2006; *Al-Ahram Weekly* (Cairo), Oct. 19-25, 2006.
47. Carter, *Palestine: Peace Not Apartheid,* p. 130-1.
48. Jimmy Carter, Sheraton Hotel, Damascus, press conference, Mar. 16, 1990.
49. Stein, *Heroic Diplomacy,* p. 255.
50. Jimmy Carter, presidential news conference, The American Presidency Project, Mar. 9, 1977

Professor Melvin Konner's letter declining involvement in a Carter advisory group:

December 26, 2006

Dr. John Hardman, M.D.
Executive Director
The Carter Center
One Copenhill
453 Freedom Parkway
Atlanta, GA 30307

Dear Dr. Hardman,

I am sorry to say that after careful and frankly painful reflection, I have decided not to participate in your group advising President Carter and The Carter Center regarding his recent book on the Middle East conflict. During our telephone conversation on December 11 (perhaps not incidentally my late father's birthday) I spoke from my heart when I agreed to participate; it is not easy for me to lose one of my greatest heroes.

In less than a week since then, events have progressed in such a way as to persuade me that I cannot in good conscience participate in such an effort.

First, President Carter has proved capable of distorting the truth about such meetings and consultations in public remarks following them. In particular, he mischaracterized the meeting he had with the executive committee of the Board of Rabbis of Greater Phoenix, saying he and they had positive interactions and prayed together, when in fact others present stated that the meeting was highly confrontational and that the prayer was merely a pro forma closing invocation. (See "Letters," *The New York Times,* Dec. 15, 2006, p. A32.) However modest my reputation may be, I will not jeopardize it by participating in a meeting that might subsequently be so starkly misconstrued.

"His repeated public insinuations that the Jews control the media and the Congress, well-worn anti-Semitic slurs that, especially coming from President Carter, present a clear and present danger to American Jews are offensive to me beyond what I can politely say."

Second, in television interviews I have seen over the past week, President Carter has revealed himself to be so rigid and inflexible in his views that he seems to me no longer capable of dialogue. In an interview with Soledad O'Brien of CNN he failed to address a single one of the criticisms she quoted from various experts in a very serious tone of voice, pointing out that she was not reading the worst of the criticisms; he began laughing inappropriately while she spoke, and when she asked him how he would respond to the criticisms he stated, "With laughter." In a number of interviews I have seen and heard him respond to highly specific questions merely by stating again and again in one form or another, "My book is completely accurate." This rigidity of thought and complete failure to engage criticisms from much greater experts than me about his numerous and serious errors of commission and omission make it clear to me that an attempt by me to advise him would be pointless and counterproductive. In addition, his repeated public insinuations that the Jews control the media and the Congress, well-worn anti-Semitic slurs that, especially coming from President Carter, present a clear and present danger to American Jews are offensive to me beyond what I can politely say.

Third, I am now carefully rereading parts of this very puzzling and problematic book, having read it through once quickly. I am not going to point out again here all the mistakes and misrepresentations pointed out by others (to take just one example, his flat contradiction of the accounts by President Clinton and Dennis Ross of events at Camp David at which they were present and he was not)—none of which he has answered—nor explain the grotesque distortion caused by his almost completely ignoring Jewish history between ancient times and 1947 (he devotes five lines on page 64 to that millennial tragic story and mentions the Holocaust twice; his "Historical Chronology" at the outset contains nothing between 1939 and 1947). However, I will call your attention to a sentence on p. 213 that had not stood out for me the first time I read it: "It is imperative that the general Arab community and all significant Palestinian groups make it clear that they will end the suicide bombings and other acts of terrorism when international laws and the ultimate goals of the Roadmap for Peace are accepted by Israel."

As someone who has lived his life as a professional reader and writer, I cannot find any way to read this sentence that does not condone the murder of Jews until such time as Israel unilaterally follows President Carter's prescription for peace. This sentence, simply put, makes President Carter an apologist for terrorists and places my children, along with all Jews everywhere, in greater danger.

When CNN's Soledad O'Brien quotes from Carter's critics, the ex-president laughs inappropriately.

"In a number of interviews I have seen and heard him respond to highly specific questions merely by stating again and again in one form or another, 'My book is completely accurate.'"

I am sure you will now understand why I cannot participate in your group advising President Carter. However, if I may, I will share this advice: If you want The Carter Center to survive and thrive independently in the future, you must take prompt and decisive steps to separate the Center from President Carter's now irrevocably tarnished legacy. You must make it clear on your web site and in appropriately circulated press releases that President Carter does not speak for The Carter Center on the subject of the Middle East conflict or the political role of the American Jewish community. If you do not do this, then President Carter's damage to his own effectiveness as a mediator, not to mention to his reputation and legacy will extend, far more tragically in my view, to The Carter Center and all its activities. Meanwhile, in my own private and modest public capacity as a university professor and writer, I will work very hard in the foreseeable future to help discredit President Carter's biased, intemperate and inflexible mischaracterizations of the reality of Israel, Palestine, terrorism, and the American Jewish community. I will urge all my colleagues and students to do the same. And, most painfully, I will discourage any connection with The Carter Center until such time as you make perfectly and publicly clear your independence from President Carter on this tragically difficult set of questions, which he has chosen so dangerously to distort and oversimplify.

I emphasize that I have been a decades-long supporter of President Carter and of The Carter Center and have defended him, his legacy, and The Center's work at every possible opportunity. It is a grave loss for me to acknowledge that this will no longer be possible.

Sincerely yours,

Melvin Konner, M.D., Ph.D.
Samuel Candler Dobbs Professor
Department of Anthropology and Program in
Neuroscience and Behavioral Biology, Emory University Departments of
Psychiatry and Neurology (by courtesy), Emory School of Medicine

Cc: Kent Alexander, Senior Vice President & General Counsel, Emory University, Steve Berman, Member, Carter Center Board of Councilors, Rabbi David Blumenthal, Ph.D., Cohen Professor of Judaic Studies, Emory University, William Branch, M.D., Carter Center Board of Councilors, Marshall Duke, Ph.D., Candler Professor of Psychology, Emory University, James W. Flannery, Ph.D., Winship Professor of Arts & Humanities, Emory University, David Hamburg, M.D., Carter Center Board of Trustees, Steven H. Hochman, Ph.D., Director, Research, Carter Center Peace Programs, The Hon. James T. Laney, Carter Center Board of Trustees, Deborah Lipstadt, Ph.D., Dorot Professor and Chair, Institute of Jewish Studies, Emory University, Gordon D. Newby, Ph.D., Professor and Chair, Middle Eastern & South Asian Studies, Emory University, Laurie Patton, Ph.D., Winship Professor and Chair, Dept. of Religion, Emory University, Robert A. Paul, Ph.D., Dean of the Faculty of Arts & Sciences, Emory University, Kenneth Stein, Ph.D., William Shatten Professor of History, Emory University

The resignation letter of 14 members of the Carter Center Advisory Board*

Fourteen members of the Carter Center advisory board have resigned after concluding that the Center's founder, former president Jimmy Carter, has turned to "malicious advocacy" for the Palestinians and against Israel.

William B. Schwartz Jr., who served as the United States Ambassador to The Bahamas during the Carter administration, is among the group.

The mass resignations come after Professor Kenneth Stein resigned his position as Middle East Fellow of the Carter Center and after Professor Melvin Konner declined a position advising Carter.

Two letters sent by the resigning members follow:

Dear fellow member of the Carter Center Board of Councilors,

This has been a difficult time for us. As members of the Board of Councilors of the Carter Center we have endeavored to promote the efforts of the Carter Center in our community. However, the recent book authored by President Carter "Palestine; Peace not Apartheid" and his comments in the press made while promoting the book have given us pause in our efforts. We are deeply troubled by the President's comments and writings and are submitting the following letter of resignation to the Carter Center. We wanted to inform you, our fellow Board members, of our actions and encourage you to contact us if you have any questions regarding our resignation.

Dear President Carter,

As members of the Board of Councilors each one of us has been proud to be associated with the Carter Center in its noble struggle to repair the world. However, in light of the publication of your latest book Palestine; Peace Not Apartheid and your subsequent comments made in promoting the book, we can no longer in good conscience continue to serve the Center as members of the Board of Councilors.

In its work in conflict resolution the Carter Center has always played the useful and constructive role of honest broker and mediator between warring parties. In your book, which portrays the conflict between Israel and

*Another member later resigned.

her neighbors as a purely one-sided affair with Israel holding all of the responsibility for resolving the conflict, you have clearly abandoned your historic role of broker in favor of becoming an advocate for one side.

The facts in dealing with the conflict are these: There are two national narratives contesting one piece of land. The Israelis, through deed and public comment, have consistently spoken of a desire to live in peace and make territorial compromise to achieve this status. The Palestinian side has consistently resorted to acts of terror as a national expression and elected parties endorsing the use of terror, the rejection of territorial compromise and of Israel's right to exist. Palestinian leaders have had chances since 1947 to have their own state, including during your own presidency when they snubbed your efforts.

Your book has confused opinion with fact, subjectivity with objectivity and force for change with partisan advocacy. Furthermore the comments you have made the past few weeks insinuating that there is a monolith of Jewish power in America are most disturbing and must be addressed by us. In our great country where freedom of expression is basic bedrock you have suddenly proclaimed that Americans cannot express their opinion on matters in the Middle East for fear of retribution from the "Jewish Lobby". In condemning the Jews of America, you also condemn Christians and others for their support of Israel. Is any interest group to

Sharon (2nd from right) and Abbas (2nd from left) meet at Sharon's home to discuss crucial issues in June 2005. The meeting was one of several summits with Sharon after Abbas became prime minister—Carter claims there were no such discussions.

be penalized for participating in the free and open political process that is America? Your book and recent comments suggest you seem to think so.

In the past you would inject yourself into this world to moderate between the two sides in the pursuit of peace and as a result you earned our admiration and support. Now you repeatedly make false claims. You wrote that UN Security Council Resolution 242 says that "Israel must withdraw from territories" (p. 38), but you know the word "must" in fact is not in the resolution. You said that since Mahmoud Abbas has been in office there have been no peace discussions. That is wrong. You wrote that Yassir Arafat told you in 1990 that, "The PLO has never advocated the annihilation of Israel" (p. 62). Given that their Charter, which explicitly calls for Israel's destruction, was not revised until the late 1990s, how could you even write such a claim as if it were credible?

You denied on Denver radio on December 12 that Palestinian Prime Minister Haniyah said he would never accept or negotiate with Israel. However the BBC monitoring service reported just the opposite. In fact Haniyah said: "We will never recognize the usurper Zionist government and will continue our jihadist movement until Bayt al-Maqdis (Jerusalem) and the Al-Aqsa Mosque are liberated. When presented with this fact you said, "No he didn't say that, no he did not do that, I did not hear that." These are not points of opinion, these are points of fact.

And finally, it is a disturbing statement to write: "that it is imperative, that the general Arab community and all significant Palestinian groups make it clear that they will end the suicide bombings and other acts of terrorism when international laws and the ultimate goals of the Roadmap for Peace are accepted by Israel." In this sentence you clearly suggest that you are condoning violence against Israelis until they do certain things (p.213). Your use of the word "Apartheid," regardless of your disclaimers, has already energized white supremacist groups who thrive on asserting Jewish control of government and foreign policy, an insinuation you made in your OPED to the LA Times on December 8, 2006: "For the last 30 years, I have witnessed and experienced the severe restraints on any free and balanced discussion of the facts." According to Web site monitoring by the Anti-Defamation League, U.S. white supremacists have enthusiastically embraced your suggestion that the Israel lobby stifles debate in this country, saying it confirms Jewish control of government and foreign policy as well as and the inherently "evil" nature of Jews. If you doubt the support you are giving and receiving, please refer to: [http://www.adl.org]

"You said that since Mahmoud Abbas has been in office there have been no peace discussions. That is wrong."

"Is any interest group to be penalized for participating in the free and open political process that is America? Your book and recent comments suggest you seem to think so."

From there you can get to the postings of four different White Supremacist organizations that both support and make use of the contents of your book and what you have said in public.

As a result it seems that you have turned to a world of advocacy, including even malicious advocacy. We can no longer endorse your strident and uncompromising position. This is not the Carter Center or the Jimmy Carter we came to respect and support. Therefore it is with sadness and regret that we hereby tender our resignation from the Board of Councilors of the Carter Center effective immediately.

Alan R. Abrams, Chairman of the Board, President and Chief Executive Officer of Servidyne, Inc.
Steve Berman, Managing Partner, OA Development.
Michael Coles, Chairman, Caribou Coffee Co.
Doug Hertz, President & CEO, United Distributors.
Jonathan Golden, Partner and Chairman, Arnall, Golden, Gregory LLP, an Atlanta law firm.
Barbara Babbit Kaufman, author.
Liane Levetan, former state senator and DeKalb CEO.
Jeff Levy, Chairman and CEO of PrDigital Media and its parent company, Biltmore Communications.
Leon Novak, Principal, The Trilogy Group.
Gail Solomon, Georgia Dome Executive Services Manager.
Cathey Steinberg, Executive Director of the Juvenile Justice Fund.
Steve Selig, President and Chairman of the Board of Selig Enterprises.
William B. Schwartz, Jr. former U.S. Ambassador to The Bahamas.
William B. Schwartz III, former senior wealth management professional at Offitbank.

Chapter 3

Promoting the Book While Refusing Debate

What's Jimmy Carter Afraid Of?

by 11 Emory professors
February 16, 2007

Once again, Jimmy Carter has shrunk from debate. Despite having written a book whose purpose he claims was to promote dialogue and discussion, he has consistently dodged appearing with anyone who could challenge him on the numerous factual errors that fill the pages of his slim book.

First it was at Brandeis University, where he was invited to appear with professor Alan Dershowitz of Harvard Law School. Dershowitz, who has written two books and numerous articles on the topic (not to mention being a respected First Amendment scholar and one of America's most distinguished attorneys), was not even allowed into the building until Carter had left.

When it became known that Carter was anxious to speak at Emory, the administration consulted a group of faculty and was advised that the most fair and academically valuable format would be to have Carter appear with someone who could engage in a productive interchange and discussion on the topic. This clearly would be the only way for the event to meet the educational standard of a leading university.

"What precisely is Carter afraid of? Could it be that Dennis Ross—who, like President Clinton, places the blame for the failure of the negotiations between the Palestinians and Israelis at Camp David II squarely on the shoulders of Yasir Arafat—would tell the former president, who blames Israel for everything, that he is simply wrong?"

Everyone agreed that the best person for this interchange was Ambassador Dennis Ross, who was the main negotiator on the Arab-Israeli situation in both the first Bush administration and the Clinton administration. He was responsible for organizing Camp David II, Clinton's last-ditch effort to find a resolution to the situation. Ross agreed to appear, but Carter pointedly refused to appear with him or with any other expert. No explanation was given.

Is this the behavior of a man who wants to promote dialogue? What precisely is Carter afraid of? Could it be that Dennis Ross—who, like President Clinton, places the blame for the failure of the negotiations between the Palestinians and Israelis at Camp David II squarely on the shoulders of Yasir Arafat—would tell the former president, who blames Israel for everything, that he is simply wrong? Remember Ross and Clinton were there; Carter was not.

The Brandeis event had sanitized pre-screened questions, no follow-up, and an audience of students clearly mesmerized by being in the presence of a former president. At least at Brandeis, Dershowitz appeared after Carter to point out that Carter's remarks (carefully scripted to appeal to the largely Jewish audience at Brandeis) were very different from what he said in the book and in numerous media events, including Al Jazeera television, where he falsely claimed that most of the critics of his book have been representatives of Jewish organizations. He has also stated on Al Jazeera that rocket barrages against Israeli homes and families are not terrorist acts. These flirtations with anti-Semitism—however unconscious—have frightened Jewish-Americans.

The *Wheel* [Emory University's student newspaper] says that it's best to let Carter have "the last word" because to do otherwise will "only prolong the debate indefinitely into the future." As if the debate will go away if Jimmy Carter is allowed a platform all by himself. Would the *Wheel* recommend that George W. Bush "be given the last word" on Iraq because to do otherwise would "prolong the debate"? The *Wheel* has joined Carter in his attempt to stifle debate even while he claims to be seeking it. A prolonged debate with a free exchange of ideas is what an academic institution is all about.

In fact, Bush, who is not known for his responsiveness to the press, has the courage to face seasoned reporters who ask tough, unscripted questions with even tougher follow-up questions. These reporters are trained to recognize when a president is dissembling, being evasive or deliberately misleading the public, and they respond accordingly.

Remember, this is a book which has been described as "moronic" (*Slate*), "strange," a "distortion" (*The New York Times*) and "cynical" with a "bait-and-switch" title (*Washington Post*). The Emory administration has thus far failed to create an event with a semblance of balance. The talk of having "someone" or a "panel on the topic" next semester is an embarrassment for an institution which proclaims that it is dedicated to "creative inquiry."

We shall absent ourselves from this staged event, which will be more a political opportunity for Carter to air his biases than an open exchange of ideas. It is unworthy of an institution with Emory's aspirations, and we have to say sadly that at this moment we are not proud of Emory.

Alan Abramowitz is the Alben W. Barkley Professor of Political Science. David R. Blumenthal is the Jay and Leslie Cohen Professor of Judaic Studies. Sander Gilman is a Distinguished Professor of the Arts and Sciences. Herbert R. Karp is an Emeritus Professor of Neurology and Medicine. Harvey Klehr is the Andrew W. Mellon Professor of Politics and History. Melvin Konner is the Samuel Candler Dobbs Professor of Anthropology. Howard I. Kushner is the Nat C. Robertson Distinguished Professor of Science and Society. Deborah E. Lipstadt is the Dorot Professor of Modern Jewish and Holocaust Studies. Andre J. Nahmias is the Richard W. Blumberg Emeritus Professor of Pediatrics. Raymond F. Schinazi is a Professor of Pediatrics and Chemistry, and the Director of the Laboratory of Biochemical Pharmacology. Donald G. Stein is the Asa G. Candler Professor of psychology, emergency medicine and neurology.

Why Won't Carter Debate His Book?

by Alan Dershowitz

You can always tell when a public figure has written an indefensible book: when he refuses to debate it in the court of public opinion. And you can always tell when he's a hypocrite to boot: when he says he wrote a book in order to stimulate a debate, and then he refuses to participate in any such debate. I'm talking about former president Jimmy Carter and his new book *Palestine: Peace Not Apartheid.*

Carter's book has been condemned as "moronic" (Slate), "anti-historical" (The Washington Post), "laughable" (San Francisco Chronicle), and riddled with errors and bias in reviews across the country. Many of the reviews have been written by non-Jewish as well as Jewish critics, and not by "representatives of Jewish organizations" as Carter has claimed. Carter has gone even beyond the errors of his book in interviews, in which he has said that the situation in Israel is worse than the crimes committed in Apartheid South Africa. When asked whether he believed that Israel's "persecution" of Palestinians was "[e]ven worse ... than a place like Rwanda," Carter answered, "Yes. I think—yes."

When Larry King referred to my review several times to challenge Carter, Carter first said I hadn't read the book and then blustered, "You know, I think it's a waste of my time and yours to quote professor Dershowitz. He's so obviously biased, Larry, and it's not worth my time to waste it on commenting on him." (He never did answer King's questions.)

The next week Carter wrote a series of op-eds bemoaning the reception his book had received. He wrote that his "most troubling experience" had been "the rejection

Alan Dershowitz addressed the Brandeis student body—after Carter conducted his own talk there, having refused to debate the Harvard professor.

of [his] offers to speak" at "university campuses with high Jewish enrollment." The fact is that Brandeis President Jehuda Reinharz had invited Carter to come to Brandeis to debate me, and Carter refused. The reason Carter gave was this: "There is no need to for me to debate somebody who, in my opinion, knows nothing about the situation in Palestine."

As Carter knows, I've been to Israel, the West Bank, and Gaza, many times—certainly more times than Carter has been there—and I've written three books dealing with the subject of Middle Eastern history, politics, and the peace process. The real reason Carter won't debate me is that I would correct his factual errors. It's not that I know too little; it's that I know too much.

Nor is Carter the unbiased observer of the Middle East that he claims to be. He has accepted money and an award from Sheik Zayed bin Sultan al-Nahyan, saying in 2001: "This award has special significance for me because it is named for my personal friend, Sheik Zayed bin Sultan al-Nahyan." This is the same Zayed, the long-time ruler of the United Arab Emirates, whose $2.5 million gift to the Harvard Divinity School was returned in 2004 due to Zayed's rampant Jew-hatred. Zayed's personal foundation, the Zayed Center, claims that it was Zionists, rather than Nazis, who "were the people who killed the Jews in Europe" during the Holocaust. It has held lectures on the blood libel and conspiracy theories about Jews and America perpetrating Sept. 11. Carter's acceptance of money from this biased group casts real doubt on his objectivity and creates an obvious conflict of interest.

Carter's refusal to debate wouldn't be so strange if it weren't for the fact that he claims that he wrote the book precisely so as to start debate over the issue of the Israel-Palestine peace process. If that were really true, Carter would be thrilled to have the opportunity to debate. Authors should be accountable for their ideas and their facts. Books shouldn't be like chapel, delivered from on high and believed on faith.

What most rankles is Carter's insistence that he is somehow brave for attacking Israel and highlighting the plight of the Palestinian people. No other conflict in the world—not even the genocides in Rwanda and Sudan—evokes more hand-wringing in the media, universities, and human rights organizations than the Israel-Palestine conflict.

Jimmy Carter isn't brave for beating up on Israel. He's a bully. And like all school-yard bullies, underneath the tough talk and bravado, there's a nagging insecurity and a fear that one day he'll have to answer for himself in a fair fight.

When Jimmy Carter's ready to speak at Brandeis, or anywhere else, I'll be there. If he refuses to debate, I will still be there—ready and willing to answer falsity with truth in the court of public opinion.

Alan Dershowitz is a professor of law at Harvard University.

This column originally appeared in the *Boston Globe*. Reprinted with permission.

"Jimmy Carter isn't brave for beating up on Israel. He's a bully. And like all school-yard bullies, underneath the tough talk and bravado, there's a nagging insecurity and a fear that one day he'll have to answer for himself in a fair fight."

Chapter 4

Religious Overtones

A Religious Problem
Jimmy Carter's book: An Israeli view

By Michael B. Oren

Several prominent scholars have taken issue with Jimmy Carter's book *Palestine: Peace Not Apartheid,* cataloguing its historical inaccuracies and lamenting its lack of balance. The journalist Jeffrey Goldberg also critiqued the book's theological purpose, which, he asserted, was to "convince American Evangelicals to reconsider their support for Israel."

Mr. Carter indeed seems to have a religious problem with the Jewish state. His book bewails the fact that Israel is not the reincarnation of ancient Judea but a modern, largely temporal democracy. "I had long taught lessons from the Hebrew Scriptures," he recalls telling Prime Minister Golda Meir during his first tour through the country. "A common historical pattern was that Israel was punished whenever the leaders turned away from devout worship of God. I asked if she was concerned about the secular nature of the Labor government."

"In revealing his unease with the idea of Jewish statehood, Mr. Carter sets himself apart from many U.S. presidents before and after him, as well as from nearly 400 years of American Christian thought. Generations of Christians in this country, representing a variety of dominations, laymen and clergy alike, have embraced the concept of renewed Jewish sovereignty in Palestine."

He complains about the fact that the kibbutz synagogue he enters is nearly empty on the Sabbath and that the Bibles presented to Israeli soldiers "was one of the few indications of a religious commitment that I observed during our visit." But he also reproves contemporary Israelis for allegedly mistreating the Samaritans—"the same complaint heard by Jesus almost two thousand years earlier"—and for pilfering water from the Jordan River, "where . . . Jesus had been baptized by John the Baptist."

Disturbed by secular Laborites, he is further unnerved by religiously minded Israelis who seek to fulfill the biblical injunction to settle the entire Land of Israel. There are "two Israels," Mr. Carter concludes, one which embodies the "the ancient culture of the Jewish people, defined by the Hebrew Scriptures," and the other in "the occupied Palestinian territories," which refuses to "respect the basic human rights of the citizens."

Whether in its secular and/or observant manifestations, Israel clearly discomfits Mr. Carter, a man who, even as president, considered himself in "full-time Christian service." Yet, in revealing his unease with the idea of Jewish statehood, Mr. Carter sets himself apart from many U.S. presidents before and after him, as well as from nearly 400 years of American Christian thought.

Generations of Christians in this country, representing a variety of dominations, laymen and clergy alike, have embraced the concept of renewed Jewish sovereignty in Palestine. The passion was already evident in 1620, when William Bradford alighted on Plymouth Rock and exclaimed, "Come, let us declare the word of God in Zion." Bradford was a leader of the Puritans, dissenting Protestants who, in their search for an unsullied religion and the strength to resist state oppression, turned to the Old Testament. There, they found a God who spoke directly to his people, who promised to deliver them from bondage and return them to their ancestral homeland. Appropriating this narrative, the Puritans fashioned themselves as the New Jews and America as their New Promised Land. They gave their children Hebrew names—David, Benjamin, Sarah, Rebecca—and called over 1,000 of their towns after Biblical places, including Bethlehem, Bethel and, of course, New Canaan.

Identifying with the Jews, a great many colonists endorsed the notion of restoring Palestine to Jewish control. Elias Boudinot, president of the Continental Congress, predicted that the Jews, "however scattered . . . are to be recovered by the mighty power of God, and restored to their beloved . . . Palestine." John Adams imagined "a hundred thousand Israelites" marching triumphantly into Palestine. "I really wish the Jews in Judea an independent nation," he wrote. During the Revolution, the association between America's struggle for independence and the Jews' struggle for repatriation was illustrated by the proposed Great Seal designed by Thomas Jefferson and Benjamin Franklin, showing Moses leading the Children of Israel toward the Holy Land.

Restorationism became a major theme in antebellum religious thought and a mainstay of the Methodist, Baptist and Presbyterian churches. In his 1844 bestseller, "The Valley of the Vision," New York University Bible scholar George Bush—a forebear of two presidents of the same name—called on the U.S. to devote its economic and military might toward re-creating a Jewish polity in Palestine. But merely envisioning such a state was insufficient for some Americans, who, in the decades before the Civil War, left home to build colonies in Palestine. Each of these settlements had the same goal: to teach the Jews, long disenfranchised from the land, to farm and so enable them to establish a modern agrarian society. In 1863, Abraham Lincoln said that "restoring the Jews to their homeland is a noble dream shared by many Americans," and that the U.S. could work to realize that goal once the Union prevailed.

Nineteenth-century restorationism reached its fullest expression in an 1891 petition submitted by Midwestern magnate William Blackstone to President Benjamin Harrison. The Blackstone Memorial, as it was called, urged the president to convene an international conference to discuss ways of reviving Jewish dominion in Palestine. Among the memorial's 400 signatories were some of America's most preeminent figures, including John D. Rockefeller, J. Pierpont Morgan, Charles Scribner and William McKinley. By the century's turn, those advocating restored Jewish sovereignty in Palestine had begun calling themselves Zionists, though the vast majority of the movement's members remained Christian rather than Jewish. "It seems to me that it is entirely proper to start a Zionist State around Jerusalem," wrote Teddy Roosevelt, "and [that] the Jews be given control of Palestine."

Such sentiments played a crucial role in gaining international recognition for Zionist claims to Palestine during World War I, when the British government sought American approval for designating that area as the Jewish national home. Though his closest counselors warned him against endorsing the move, Woodrow Wilson, the son and grandson of Presbyterian preachers, rejected their advice. "To think that I the son of the manse [parsonage] should be able to help restore the Holy Land to its people," he explained. With Wilson's imprimatur, Britain issued the declaration that became the basis of its League of Nations mandate in Palestine, and as the precursor to the 1947 U.N. Partition Resolution creating the Jewish state.

The question of whether or not to recognize that state fell to Harry S. Truman. Raised in a Baptist household where he learned much of the Bible by heart, Truman had been a member of the pro-Zionist American Christian Palestine Committee and an advocate of the right of Jews—particularly Holocaust survivors—to immigrate to Palestine. He was naturally inclined to acknowledge the nascent state but encountered fervid opposition from the entire foreign policy establishment. If America sided with the Zionists, officials in the State and Defense departments cautioned, the Arabs would cut off oil supplies to the West, undermine America's economy, and expose Europe to Soviet invasion. Hundreds of thousands of U.S. troops would have to be sent to Palestine to save its Jews from massacre.

Truman listened carefully to these warnings and then, at 6:11 on the evening of May 14, he announced that the U.S. would be the first nation to recognize the newly declared State of Israel. While the decision may have stemmed in part from domestic political considerations, it is difficult to conceive that any politician, much less one of Truman's character, would have risked global catastrophe by recognizing a frail and miniscule country. More likely, the dramatic démarche reflected Truman's religious background and his commitment to the restorationist creed. Introduced a few weeks later to an American Jewish delegation as the president who had helped create Israel, Truman took umbrage and snapped, "What you mean 'helped create'? I am Cyrus"—a reference to the Persian king who returned the Jews from exile—"I am Cyrus!"

Since 1948, some administrations (Eisenhower, Bush Sr.) have been less ardent in their attachment to Israel, and others (Kennedy, Nixon) more so. Throughout the last 60 years, though, the U.S. has never wavered in its concern for Israel's survival and its support for the Jewish people's right to statehood. While U.S.–Israel ties are no doubt strengthened by common bonds of democracy and Western culture, religion remains an integral component in that relationship. We know that Lyndon Johnson's Baptist grandfather told him to "take care of the Jews, God's chosen people," and that Bill Clinton's pastor, on his deathbed, made the future president promise never to abandon the Jewish state. We know how faith has impacted the policies of George W. Bush, who is perhaps the most pro-Israel president in history.

In his apparent attempt to make American Christians rethink their affection for Israel, Jimmy Carter is clearly departing from time-honored practice. This has not been the legacy of evangelicals alone, but of many religious denominations in the U.S., and not solely the conviction of Mr. Bush, but of generations of American leaders. In the controversial title of his book, Mr. Carter implicitly denounces Israel for its separatist policies, but, by doing so, he isolates himself from centuries of American tradition.

Mr. Oren is a senior fellow at the Shalem Center in Jerusalem.

Carter's Faith: Habitat for Hostility

By Dexter Van Zile

Despite the factual errors in his book, *Palestine: Peace Not Apartheid,*[1] former president Jimmy Carter enjoys a reservoir of credibility as a commentator on the Arab-Israeli conflict. This credibility is in part a consequence of his reputation as a devout and thoughtful Christian. In particular, President Carter's involvement with Habitat for Humanity, a Christian organization that builds homes for the poor, and his devotion to Maranatha Baptist Church in Plains, Georgia, where he has taught adult Bible classes since 1982, have burnished his reputation as a man of faith and good intentions.

Admiration for Carter cuts across denominational boundaries. Father Robert Drinan, a Roman Catholic priest, lauded Carter's 1996 book, *Living Faith,* in reverential terms, writing that Carter is "a Christian who accepts the Bible as the word of God and the person of Christ as the greatest grace God has given to all his sons and daughters."[2]

President Carter's reputation as a thoughtful, progressive Christian was cemented by his decision to disassociate himself from the Southern Baptist Convention (while still remaining a member of his local church) in 2000 over what he called the denomination's "increasingly rigid" doctrines, particularly those regarding women in the pulpit.[3] His decision to leave the SBC generated an outpouring of support from liberal Christians in the U.S. For example, the *Atlanta-Journal Constitution* published numerous letters to the editor supporting his decision, one of which compared Carter's break with the SBC with the fall of the Berlin Wall.[4] Despite the controversy, his decision to leave the SBC elicited an expression of sadness from the denomination's theologically conservative president, Rev. James Merritt, who called the former president "a man of sincere faith."[5]

"Because of his reputation as a well-intentioned Christian, commentators tend to downplay, excuse, or completely ignore the factual misstatements in the text."

Respect for Carter as a devout Christian has proven to be a powerful asset for the former president in the debate about his latest book. Because of his reputation as a well-intentioned Christian, commentators tend to downplay, excuse, or completely ignore the factual misstatements in the text. For example, Charles Kimball, writing in the April 1, 2007 issue of *Sojourners,* a magazine for progressive Christians, acknowledged errors in *Palestine: Peace Not Apartheid,* but refrained from offering robust criticism for these errors. After acknowledging that a passage on page 213 of Carter's book "can be taken to imply that terrorism and suicide bombings have validity," Kimball writes:

> Although the book and Carter's life work leave no doubt that he denounces terrorism, he acknowledged at Brandeis that this sentence was a serious mistake, "improper and stupid" in its working, and promised that all future editions will be corrected.

Palestine: Peace Not Apartheid is framed by Carter's orientation as a Baptist with deep emotional and religious roots in the Holy Land. As an unapologetic follower of Jesus, Carter takes seriously the call to be an agent of reconciliation in a broken and hurting world.[6]

Kimball then contrasts Carter with John Hagee, founder of Christians United for Israel, a "pre-millenial dispensationalist who argues fervently that we are in the shadow of the end times." In short, Kimball invokes Carter's religious beliefs to put his errors into a sympathetic context and then to distinguish him from Christians like Hagee, whom he condemns for his "uncritical" support for Israel.

"While commentators are willing to give the former president's factual errors a pass because of his religious beliefs, they seem uninterested in assessing how his Christian beliefs 'undergird' his attitude toward the modern state of Israel."

Another example of how Carter's reputation as a devout Christian was used to distract attention from the errors in his book took place when Krista Tippett, a radio host for American Public Media's "Speaking of Faith," interviewed Carter on April 26, 2007. During the interview, Tippett refrained from challenging him about the errors, stating: "Jimmy Carter has discussed this controversy at length and apologized in part. I decided not to retrace the ground in the limited time I had with him. Instead, I wanted to get a sense of the basic Christianity that formed Jimmy Carter and has undergirded his actions in the White House and since."[7]

While commentators are willing to give the former president's factual errors a pass because of his religious beliefs, they seem uninterested in assessing how his Christian beliefs "undergird" his attitude toward the modern state of Israel. While Carter is no pre-millenial dispensationalist, his writings make it perfectly clear that Biblical depictions of ancient Israel still figure prominently in his religious imagination, and color his views of the modern state of Israel.

When Yitzhak Rabin invited Carter to Israel in 1973, Carter, who was then serving as Governor of Georgia and quietly preparing for his 1976 run for the Presidency, responded enthusiastically.

> Having studied Bible lessons since early childhood and taught them for twenty years, I was infatuated with the Holy Land, and my wife, Rosalyn, and I arranged to accept his invitation in 1973. In preparing for this trip, we pored over maps and reviewed both the ancient and modern history of Israel. Our choice of how to spend the ten-day visit was a series of compromises because I was torn between the pleasure of visiting the Christian holy places I had always longed to see and the knowledge that I should concentrate on preparing for another political career. (*Palestine: Peace Not Apartheid,* page 22).

Carter's infatuation with the Holy Land differs from that of Christian Zionists. Unlike Hagee, Carter has repeatedly called for Israel to withdraw from the Gaza Strip and the West Bank (which Hagee regards as God-given to the Jewish people). Nevertheless, he does believe that God has indeed given some portion of land in the Middle East to the Jewish people. In a Nov. 16, 2006 interview with Jennifer Siegel writing for Forward.com, Carter stated that his belief is "that God ordained that the Jews should have a homeland there, and I think that international law beginning in 1948 says the same exact thing, and that's what I believe."[8]

But like pre-millenial dispensationalists with whom he disagrees about Israel's presence in the West Bank, Carter regards the Jewish homeland as contingent on the faithfulness of its people and leaders to the rules that come with God's promise of land outlined in the Hebrew Scriptures. In an extended passage in *The Blood of Abraham,* his 1985 book on the Arab-Israeli conflict, Carter recounts the story of ancient Israel, laying particular emphasis on the requirements that come with the land of Israel.

> God promised David that because of his faithfulness, his kingdom would be established forever.
>
> However, Moses had made it clear to the Israelites that God's promises always obliged his chosen people to be obedient and faithful to the covenant and divine law. David and his son Solomon had many successors, almost all of them disobedient, under whom the land was ruled as two separate nations, Judah and Israel. Both nations failed to meet God's standards of loyalty and justice and so were destroyed by their enemies, Israel in about 722 B.C. and Judah in about 586 B.C. The Jews were taken into captivity, but some of them subsequently returned to Jerusalem, where they lived under foreign domination but were able to preserve their customs and religious faith. (*The Blood of Abraham,* page 7)

It is important to note that Carter's history leaves out an important fact: Jews, after returning from the Babylonian Captivity, did not always live under foreign domination. They were independent from the time of the Hasmonean rebellion until the Jewish kingdom's subjugation to Rome; a period of about a century.[10]

"Others have what is generally recognized as a virtually universal 'right of self-determination.' In contrast, Jews are entitled to their state, in Carter's view, only if they adhere to the obedience and faithfulness to which they are enjoined in the Hebrew Bible."

In any event, in both *The Blood of Abraham,* and *Palestine: Peace Not Apartheid* Carter makes it clear that, to his thinking, the rules that come with the promise of land to the Jews are not moral principles that should be followed by all of humanity, but are still-operative principles used to assess modern Israeli society. In essence, he distinguishes the Jews' claim to a state as different from that of any other ethnic/national community. Others have what is generally recognized as a virtually universal "right of self-determination." In contrast, Jews are entitled to their state, in Carter's view, only if they adhere to the obedience and faithfulness to which they are enjoined in the Hebrew Bible. Moreover, Carter sets himself up as the judge of that obedience and faithfulness.

In *The Blood of Abraham,* Carter recounts his dismay at the lack of religious interest at Ayelet Hashahar, a kibbutz in northern Galilee he visited during his 1973 trip.

> It was the Sabbath, and we asked if we could attend the worship service. At the appointed time we entered the synagogue and stood quietly just inside the door. There were only two other worshipers. When I asked if this was typical, our guide gave a wry smile and shrugged his shoulders as if it was not important either way. (*The Blood of Abraham, page 23*)

A few pages later, he describes how he raised the issue of Israel's apparent faithlessness at a meeting with Prime Minister Golda Meir:

> She was not pressed with state business that morning so we stayed for an extended talk. When she asked if we had any concerns, I replied that there was one of a religious nature that I hesitated to mention. I knew that she had been born in Russia and that neither she nor the key members of her cabinet were known to be devout Jews. With a smile she encouraged me to go on, and I told her about the sabbath (sic) service at Ayelet Hashahar and a general absence of religious interest among the Israelis. I commented that during biblical times, the Israelites triumphed when they were close to God and were defeated when unfaithful. She laughed aloud and agreed with me, but added that this was not a matter of concern to her because there were certainly enough "orthodox" Jews around. She was referring to the religious Jews in the Israeli parliament, who were sometimes a real thorn in her side. She added, "If you attend a session of the Knesset, you will see them in action and will know that they have not lost their faith." With Israel's system of elections, which necessitates a coalition of parties to form a ruling majority, the minority religious parties had an influence far exceeding their numerical strength. (*The Blood of Abraham, pages 27–28*)

In *Palestine: Peace Not Apartheid,* Carter describes his statements to Meir regarding Israel's religious obligations in a much more pointed manner.

> With some hesitation, I said that I had long taught lessons from the Hebrew Scriptures and that a common historical pattern was that Israel was punished whenever the leaders turned away from devout worship of God. I asked if she was concerned about the secular nature of her Labor government. She seemed surprised at my temerity and dismissed my comments with a shrug and a laugh. She lit one cigarette from another and then said that "orthodox" Jews still existed and could assume that portion of the nation's responsibility. She was referring to the religious Jews in the Israeli parliament, who were sometimes a real thorn in her side. She added, "If you attend a session of the Knesset, you will see them in action and will know that they have not lost their faith." With Israel's system of elections, which necessitates a collation of parties to form a ruling majority, the minority religious organizations had an influence far exceeding their numerical strength. (*Palestine: Peace Not Apartheid, pages 31–32*)

These passages reveal a troubling mixture of Christian entitlement and inconsistency. Carter, as a Christian, feels, again, perfectly free to assess the legitimacy of the modern state of Israel against a metric of fidelity to the Jewish faith, even as he bemoans the undue influence of Orthodox Jews on Israeli politics. Also, he once more sets himself up as the judge of Jewish fidelity to the Jewish faith. In addition, his criteria for that fidelity are selective. For example, a substantial part of Biblical injunction entails Temple ritual. Would Carter argue that the Jews of Israel are remiss because, having regained control of the Temple Mount in 1967, they have not rebuilt the Temple and reinstituted Temple ritual?

This not only illustrates President Carter's selectivity in setting himself up as the judge of Jewish religious duties and obligations that, to his thinking, are essential to Jews' deserving their state, but underscores Carter's denying Israelis

"The lessons, recorded in 1998 and released under the title 'Sunday Mornings in Plains, Bible Studies with Jimmy Carter: Leading a Worthy Life,' reveal a troubling tendency to use Judaism as a negative backdrop to highlight the positive attributes of Christianity."

the right to determine for themselves how they will follow the dictates of their conscience—a right of conscience he readily accorded himself when, for example, in 2000, he left the Southern Baptist Convention. For Carter, the Jews are not a people like any other, but a people beholden to a special obligation to be faithful—in a manner of his construing—to the God of the Old Testament.

Carter is not unique in this attitude. In 1984, A. Roy Eckhart, a commentator on Christian-Jewish relations, condemned the Christian impulse to fabricate Jews into "special witness of God whether they like it or not."

> If Jews wish to opt for a religious identity, fine—and the same goes for their dereligionization. One way or the other, the determination is exclusively theirs, not that of Christians.[11]

A further irony is that for President Carter, Israel's legitimacy is dependent on adherence to a religion toward which he has exhibited a troubling suspicion. Carter's attitude towards Judaism is readily apparent in recordings of Carter's Bible lessons at Maranatha Baptist Church in Plains, Georgia published by Simon and Schuster in 2007. The lessons, recorded in 1998 and released under the title "Sunday Mornings in Plains, Bible Studies with Jimmy Carter: Leading a Worthy Life," reveal a troubling tendency to use Judaism as a negative backdrop to highlight the positive attributes of Christianity.

For example, Carter speaks at length about Jewish hostility toward Christians and Samaritans and how Apostle Paul targeted believers in Christ for death or imprisonment. "This was Paul's reason for existence. His total commitment was to abolish this blight on humanity—gentiles who claimed to have an acceptable relationship with God almighty," he says.

Carter also speaks about how Christ was almost killed by his "own hometown people" for detailing how "the ancient prophets had blessed non-Jews" and about how Christ was only thanked by the one non-Jewish leper out of a group of 10 he had healed. He also describes Jewish rules of ritual purity in a manner that portrays first century Jews as parochial, suspicious bigots. "If a Jew married a gentile, that person was considered to be dead," he states. "If a Jew went into the home of a gentile, that Jew was considered to be what? Unclean and had to go through a religious ceremony to become cleansed again so that they could even worship in the Temple."

Carter states that his intent is not to criticize Jews, "but we're just trying to point out the historical change, the transforming change that took place when Jesus came." Nevertheless, the negative references give a jaundiced, mean-spirited distortion of actual Jewish practice and create an image of a parochial and hostile people who bristle at being reminded of the higher principles of their faith.

To be sure, Carter acknowledges that Christians have behaved in a divisive manner toward one another, but even this acknowledgement is followed by an emphasis on just how far outside the pale Jews are from the rest of humanity. When talking about how different the world would be if Protestants and Catholics, conservatives and liberals, Amish and Mennonites could get together and mend their difference, Carter adds "If we could reach out with love, even for Jews."

Carter is not the only Christian commentator to set Judaism up as a negative backdrop against which he then highlights the superiority of Christ and of Christianity. Amy-Jill Levine has written extensively about this tendency in her book, *The Misunderstood Jew.*[12] Christian preachers and theologians have long used negative and inaccurate caricatures of Judaism to highlight the superiority of their own faith. In particular, Levine writes that Jews have been portrayed as "narrow, clannish, particularistic, and xenophobic, whereas Jesus and the church are engaged in universal outreach."[13]

Levine points out a telling contradiction on the part of many progressive Christian commentators.

> Ironically, when Jews in the New Testament are seen as wanting to preserve their own traditions, of diet and circumcision, of synagogue practice and forms of worship, Christian readers are sometimes inclined to regard these efforts as retrograde or exclusive. Today, when any other ethnic or religious group seeks to maintain its own integrity despite cultural pressures to assimilation, it is regarded positively as promoting identity, resisting colonialism, and celebrating its heritage. (*The Misunderstood Jew,* page 159)

Clearly, Carter's assessment of first century Judaism colors his view of the modern state of Israel and its leaders. For example, in *The Blood of Abraham,* Carter portrays Menachem Begin as a devout, but territorial Jew indifferent to the common bonds of the three Abrahamic faiths.

> A dedicated student of the Bible, on occasion he quoted scriptural passages, such as "If I forget thee, O Jerusalem, let my right hand forget her cunning," in order to emphasize why he would not share authority in Jerusalem. I do not recall any occasion, however, when he initiated a discussion about Christianity or Islam or participated in any comparative analysis of religious beliefs. In fact, Sadat's comments seem to cause Begin some slight embarrassment. (*Blood of Abraham,* page 9)

This is not the only instance in which Carter's opinion of modern Israel dovetails perfectly with his attitude toward first century Judaism. In *Palestine: Peace Not Apartheid,* Carter draws a straight line between the misdeeds of first century Jews and the misdeeds of modern Israel. Describing his 1973 trip to Israel Carter writes:

> It was especially interesting to visit with some of the few surviving Samaritans, who complained to us that their holy sites and culture were not being respected by Israeli authorities—the same complaint heard by Jesus and his disciples almost two thousand years earlier. (*Palestine: Peace Not Apartheid,* page 7)

This passage drew a justified rebuke from Jeffrey Goldberg, who in the *Wash-*

"Rather than invoke Carter's religious beliefs to excuse or minimize the factual errors in *Palestine: Peace Not Apartheid* (which invariably cut against Israel), Christian commentators should consider the possibility that Carter's religiously cloaked biases against Jews and Judaism actually motivate those errors."

ington Post wrote that "There are, of course, no references to 'Israeli authorities' in the Christian Bible. Only a man who sees Israel as a lineal descendant of the Pharisees could write such a sentence."[14]

Sadly, Goldberg is right. Rather than invoke Carter's religious beliefs to excuse or minimize the factual errors in *Palestine: Peace Not Apartheid* (which invariably cut against Israel), Christian commentators should consider the possibility that Carter's religiously cloaked biases against Jews and Judaism actually motivate those errors.

Dexter Van Zile is Christian Media Analyst at CAMERA.

1. New York: Simon and Schuster, 2006 (288 pp. $27).
2. Robert Drinan, "Living Faith" (book review), *National Catholic Reporter,* May 30, 1997.
3. White, Gayle, "Carter cuts ties to 'rigid' Southern Baptists," Cox News Service, Oct. 19, 2000.
4. Richard Waller, "Baptist Convention an oppressive body," *The Atlanta Journal Constitution,* Oct. 25, 2000.
5. White, Gayle, "Carter cuts ties to 'rigid' Southern Baptists," Cox News Service, Oct. 19, 2000.
6. Charles Kimball, "Road Map to Peace – Or Destruction? Three Evangelicals on the challenges of Israel-Palestine," *Sojourners,* April 2007.
7. Krista Tippett (host), "The Private Faith of Jimmy Carter," American Public Radio, Speaking of Faith, April 26, 2007.
8. Jennifer Siegel, "Carter Discusses New Book on Israel and the Middle East," Forward.com, Nov. 16. 2006.
9. Fayetteville, University of Arkansas Press, 1993.
10. Raymond P. Scheindlin, *A Short History of the Jewish People,* Oxford University Press, 1998, p. 39.
11. A. Roy Eckhardt, "Anti-Semitism is the Heart," *Theology Today,* October, 1984.
12. San Francisco: HarperSanFrancisco, 2007 (258 pp. $24.95)
13. Levine, The Misunderstood Jew, p. 125.
14. Jeffrey Goldberg, "What Would Jimmy Do?" *The Washington Post,* Dec. 10, 2006.

Chapter 5

Arab Funding of the Carter Center

Carter's Arab Funders

Jimmy Carter's dependence on Arab funding stretches back to early business connections in the 1970's and continues in the present with multi-million dollar donations to his richly-endowed Carter Center in Atlanta, Georgia. The Center's 2006 Annual Report reveals total net assets of $412,393,757, a strikingly large figure for a non-profit organization.

Among donors listed giving more than a million dollars are His Royal Highness Prince Alawaleed Bin Talal Bin Abdulaziz Al Saud Fund, the Sultanate of Oman, Bakr M. BinLadin for the Saudi BinLadin Group, the Saudi Fund for Development and the Government of the United Arab Emirates. His Royal Highness Prince Abdullah Bin Mosaad Bin Abdul Aziz, His Royal Highness Prince Moulay Hicham Ben Abdallah and others are also listed as lavish supporters of the Center.

Saudi Crown Prince Abdullah Bin Mosa'ad Bin Abdulaziz Al Saud is listed among donors to the Carter Center.

Carter's obsessive denigration of Israel and his virtual silence—along with that of his Center—about widespread human rights abuses in the same Arab states whose leading figures are among his most munificent contributors, raise obvious questions about his motives and integrity. Saudi Arabia, for instance, is categorized by Freedom House, the non-governmental group that yearly assesses freedom in nations of the world, as among the "Worst of the Worst." According to their indices, Saudi Arabia is a repressive society with no political parties, no religious freedom, no freedom of speech, no freedom of assembly, no independent judiciary and severe limitations on women—who cannot vote, drive or participate equally in most aspects of society.

Freedom House includes Saudi Arabia in its "Worst of the worst: The World's Most Repressive Societies" but the Carter Center's Human Rights program has almost nothing to say about the kingdom.

Ironically, Carter's distorted assault on Israel has echoed the conspiratorial tack of that nation's most fanatical detractors, stressing an alleged chilling influence on public debate exerted by its U.S. supporters. In particular, he charges that criticism of the supposedly "abominable oppression and persecution" inflicted by Israel on the Palestinians is stifled by "the extraordinary lobbying efforts of the American-Israel Political Action Committee (sic)."[1]

Yet the reported hundreds of millions of dollars from Saudi and Gulf contributors that have flowed into the Carter Center as well as the vast sums of Arab money donated to American universities, think tanks, lobbies, religious institutions and other opinion-shaping institutions elicit no concern whatever from Jimmy Carter about Arab influence on American foreign policy. The publication of *Palestine: Peace Not Apartheid* has underscored the ideological alliance of Carter and the Arab plutocrats whose views he reflects and advances.

1. *Los Angeles Times* December 8, 2006

Carter's Arab Financiers

By Rachel Ehrenfeld
December 21, 2006

To understand what feeds former president Jimmy Carter's anti-Israeli frenzy, look at his early links to Arab business. Between 1976-1977, the Carter family peanut business received a bailout in the form of a $4.6 million, "poorly managed" and highly irregular loan from the National Bank of Georgia (NBG). According to a July 29, 1980 Jack Anderson expose in *The Washington Post,* the bank's biggest borrower was Mr. Carter, and its chairman at that time was Mr. Carter's confidant, and later his director of the Office of Management and Budget, Bert Lance.

At that time, Mr. Lance's mismanagement of the NBG got him and the bank into trouble. Agha Hasan Abedi, the Pakistani founder of the Bank of Credit and Commerce International (BCCI), known as the bank "which would bribe God," came to Mr. Lance's rescue making him a $100,000-a-year consultant. Abedi then declared: "We would never talk about exploiting his relationship with the president." Next, he introduced Mr. Lance to Saudi billionaire Gaith Pharaon, who fronted for BCCI and the Saudi royal family. In January 1978, Abedi paid off Mr. Lance's $3.5 million debt to the NBG, and Pharaon secretly gained control over the bank.

Mr. Anderson wrote: "Of course, the Saudis remained discretely silent... kept quiet about Carter's irregularities... [and] renegotiated the loan to Carter's advantage."

There is no evidence that the former president received direct payment from the Saudis. But "according to... the bank files, [it] renegotiated the repayment terms... savings... $60,000 for the Carter family... The President owned 62% of the business and therefore was the largest beneficiary." Pharaon later contributed generously to the former president's library and center.

Saudi billionaire Prince Alwaleed bin Talal is another Saudi donor to Carter's Center.

Mr. Lance introduced Mr. Carter to Abedi, the latter gave $500,000 to help the former president establish his center at Emory University. Later, Abedi contributed more than $10 million to Mr. Carter's different projects. Even after BCCI was indicted—and convicted—for drug money laundering, Mr. Carter accepted $1.5 million from Abedi, his "good friend."

A quick survey of the major contributors to the Carter Center reveals hundreds of millions of dollars from Saudi and Gulf contributors. But it was BCCI that helped Mr. Carter established his center.

BCCI's origins were primarily ideological. Abedi wanted the bank to reflect the supra-national Muslim credo and "the best bridge to help the world of Islam, and the best way to fight the evil influence of the Zionists." Shortly after assuming office, in March 1977, Mr. Carter made his first public statement regarding a Palestinian "homeland." Since then, he has devoted much of his time to denouncing Israel's self-defense against Palestinian terrorism, which he claims is not only "abominable oppression and persecution" of the Palestinians, but also damages U.S. interests in the region.

By the time BCCI was shut down in July 1991, it operated in 73 countries with a deficit of $12 billion, which it had managed to hide with wealthy Arab shareholders and Western luminaries. Among them Sheikh Zayed bin Sultan al-Nahayan of Abu Dhabi, who gave hundreds of millions of dollars to Yasser Arafat and Palestinian terrorist groups, and who branded the United States: "our enemy number one"; Former head of Saudi foreign intelligence service, and King Faisal's brother-in-law, Kamal Adham—who with another Saudi, the banker of the royal family, Khaled bin Mahfouz, staged BCCI's attempt to illegally purchase the Washington-based First American bank, in the early 1980s.

True to its agenda, BCCI assisted in spreading and strengthening the Islamic message; they enabled Pakistan's nuclear ambitions, and helped the Palestinian leadership to amass a $10 billion-plus fortune, used to further terrorist activities and to buy more influence in the West.

BCCI founders also supported the Islamic fundamentalist opposition to the Shah of Iran, and saw it as an opportunity to undermine Western influence in the Gulf. They assisted the revolution financially, reinforcing their position within the leadership of the Iranian revolution. Ironically, the success of that revolution cost Mr. Carter his presidency.

BCCI's money also facilitated the Saudi agenda to force Israel to recognize Palestinians "rights," convincing Egyptian president Anwar Sadat to sign the Camp David Accords in September 1978. Since then, Mr. Carter repeatedly provided legitimacy to Arafat's corrupt regime, and now, like the Saudis, he even sides with homicidal Hamas as the "legitimate" representative of the Palestinian people.

In a recent interview with the *Los Angeles Times,* Mr. Carter again laid responsibility for U.S. bias against the destitute, depressed and (consequently) violent Palestinians on American policy makers' helplessness, over the last 30 years, against the menacing tactics of the powerful American-Israel Political Affairs Committee (AIPAC).

However, it seems that AIPAC's real fault was its failure to outdo the Saudi's purchases of the former president's loyalty. "There has not been any nation in the world that has been more cooperative than Saudi Arabia," the *New York Times* quoted Mr. Carter June 1977, thus making the Saudis a major factor in U. S. foreign policy.

Evidently, the millions in Arab petrodollars feeding Mr. Carter's global endeavors, often in conflict with U.S. government policies, also ensure his loyalty.

This column originally appeared in the *Washington Times.*
Reprinted with permission, Rachel Ehrenfeld, Director of the American Center for Democracy.

Ex-President for Sale

By Alan M. Dershowitz
January 15, 2007

It now turns out that Jimmy Carter—who is accusing the Jews of buying the silence of the media and politicians regarding criticism of Israel—has been bought and paid for by Arab money. In his recent book tour to promote *Palestine: Peace Not Apartheid,* Carter has been peddling a particularly nasty bit of bigotry. The canard is that Jews own and control the media, and prevent newspapers and the broadcast media from presenting an objective assessment of the Arab-Israeli conflict, and that Jews have bought and paid for every single member of Congress so as to prevent any of them from espousing a balanced position. How else can anyone understand Carter's claims that it is impossible for the media and politicians to speak freely about Israel and the Middle East? The only explanation—and one that Carter tap dances around, but won't come out and say directly—is that Jews control the media and buy politicians. Carter then presents himself as the sole heroic figure in American public life who is free of financial constraints to discuss Palestinian suffering at the hands of the Israelis.

Listen carefully to what Carter says about the media: the plight of the Palestinians is "not something that has been acknowledged or even discussed in this country... You never hear anything about what is happening to the Palestinians by the Israelis." He claims to have personally "witnessed and experienced the severe restraints on any free and balanced discussion of the facts." He implies that the Jews impose these "severe restraints." He then goes on to say that the only reason his book—which has been universally savaged by reviewers—is receiving such negative reviews is because they are all being written by "representatives of Jewish organizations" (demonstrably false!). So much for the media.

Now here is what he says about politicians:

"It would be almost politically suicidal for members of Congress to espouse a balanced position between Israel and Palestine, to suggest that Israel comply with international law or to speak in defense of justice or human rights for Palestinians. Very few would ever deign to visit the Palestinian cities of Ramallah, Nablus, Hebron, Gaza City or even Bethlehem and talk to the beleaguered residents."

Each of these claims is demonstrably false. The plight of the Palestinians has been covered more extensively, per capita, than the plight of any other group in the world, certainly more than the Tibetans and the victims of genocides in Darfur and Rwanda. Moreover, Carter totally ignores the impact of Arab oil money and the influence of the Saudi lobby. In numerous instances where the Arab lobbies have been pitted against the Israeli lobby, the former has prevailed.

Even beyond these nasty canards, the big story that the media and political figures in America have missed is how grievously they, themselves have been insulted and disrespected by our self-righteous former president. Carter is lecturing *The New York Times, The Washington Post, the Los Angeles Times,* CNN, and the major networks about how they are incapable of reporting the news objectively because they are beholden to some Jewish cabal. He is telling Pulitzer Prize winning writers such as Tom Friedman and Samatha Power that they did not deserve their prizes. He is telling George Will that his reporting is controlled by his Jewish bosses (sound a little bit like Judith Regan?). And he is denying that Anderson Cooper is capable of filing an honest report from the West Bank.

As far as our legislators are concerned, he is accusing Barack Obama, John McCain, Hillary Clinton, and Patrick Leahy of being bought and paid for by the Israeli lobby. On Planet Carter, even congressmen with no Jewish constituents would be committing political suicide by taking a balanced position on the Middle East. What an outrageous insult to some of the best journalists and most independent political figures in the world.

At the bottom, Carter is saying that no objective journalist or politician could actually believe that America's support for Israel is based on moral and strategic considerations and not on their own financial self-interest. Such a charge is so insulting to every honest legislator and journalist in this country that I am amazed that Carter has been let off the hook so easily. Only the self-righteous Jimmy Carter is capable of telling the truth, because only he is free of financial pressures that might influence his positions.

It now turns out that the shoe is precisely on the other foot. Recent disclosures prove that it is Carter who has been bought and paid for by anti-Israel Arab and Islamic money.

Zayed's personal foundation, the Zayed Center, claims that it was Zionists, rather than Nazis, who "were the people who killed the Jews in Europe" during the Holocaust.

Carter accepted a $500,000 gift from Sheikh Zayed bin Sultan al-Nahyan, president of the United Arab Emirates, whose Zayed Center promoted anti-Semitism and Holocaust denial.

Journalist Jacob Laskin has documented the tens of millions of dollars that the Carter Center has accepted from Saudi Arabian royalty and assorted other Middle Eastern sultans, who, in return, Carter dutifully praised as peaceful and tolerant (no matter how despotic the regime). And these are only the confirmed, public donations.

Carter has also accepted half a million dollars and an award from Sheik Zayed bin Sultan al-Nahyan, saying in 2001: "This award has special significance for me because it is named for my personal friend, Sheik Zayed bin Sultan al-Nahyan." This is the same Zayed, the long-time ruler of the United Arab Emirates, whose $2.5 million gift to the Harvard Divinity School was returned in 2004 due to Zayed's rampant Jew-hatred. Zayed's personal foundation, the Zayed Center, claims that it was Zionists, rather than Nazis, who "were the people who killed the Jews in Europe" during the Holocaust. It has held lectures on the blood libel and conspiracy theories about Jews and America perpetrating Sept. 11.

Another journalist, Rachel Ehrenfeld, in a thorough and devastating article on "Carter's Arab Financiers" meticulously catalogues Carter's ties to Arab moneymen, from a Saudi bailout of his peanut farm in 1976, to funding for Carter's presidential library, to continued support for all manner of Carter's post-presidential activities. For instance, it was the Bank of Credit and Commerce International (BCCI), founded in Pakistan and fronted by a Saudi billionaire, Gaith Pharaon, that helped Carter start up his beloved Carter Center. According to Ehrenfeld:

"BCCI's origins were primarily ideological. [Agha Hasan] Abedi wanted the bank to reflect the supra-national Muslim credo and 'the best bridge to help the world of Islam, and the best way to fight the evil influence of the Zionists.'

As Ehrenfeld concluded:

> "[I]t seems that AIPAC's real fault was its failure to outdo the Saudi's purchases of the former president's loyalty. There has not been any nation in the world that has been more cooperative than Saudi Arabia," *The New York Times* quoted Mr. Carter June 1977, thus making the Saudis a major factor in U. S. foreign policy.
>
> Evidently, the millions in Arab petrodollars feeding Mr. Carter's global endeavors, often in conflict with U.S. government policies, also ensure his loyalty.

It is particularly disturbing that a former president who has accepted dirty blood-money from dictators, anti-Semites, Holocaust deniers, and supporters of terrorism should try to deflect attention from his own conflicts of interest by raising the oldest canard in the sordid history of anti-Semitism: namely, that Jews have dual loyalty and use their money improperly to influence the country they live in, in favor of the country to which they owe their real allegiance. Abraham Foxman responded to Carter's canard as follows:

> As disturbing as Carter's simplistic approach is, however, even more disturbing is his picking up on the Mearsheimer -Walt theme of Jewish control of American policy, though in much more abbreviated form and not being the focus of his work. Referring to U.S. policy and the "condoning" of Israel's actions, Carter says: "There are constant and vehement political and media debates in Israel concerning its policies in the West Bank but because of powerful political, economic, and religious forces in the U.S., Israeli government decisions are rarely questioned or condemned, voices from Jerusalem dominate our media, and most American citizens are unaware of circumstances in the occupied territories." In other words, the old canard and conspiracy theory of Jewish control of the media, Congress, and the U.S. government is rearing its ugly head in the person of a former President.

As noted above, the most perverse aspect of Carter's foray into bigotry is that as he pours this old wine into new bottles he is himself awash in Arab money. When a politician levels these kinds of cynical accusations against others, it would seem incumbent on him to show that his own hands are clean and his own pockets empty.

Accordingly I now call upon Carter to make full public disclosure of all of his and the Carter Center's ties to Arab money. If he fails to do so, I challenge the media to probe deeply into his, his family's, and his Center's Arab ties so that the public can see precisely the sources and amounts of money he has received and judge whether it has corrupted the process of objective reportage and politics by Carter and others who have received such funds. Finally, I ask the appropriate government agencies to conduct an investigation into whether Carter should be required to register as a lobbyist for foreign interests.

Let's stop invoking discredited ethnic stereotypes, look at the hard facts, and actually see who's being bought and sold.

Alan Dershowitz is a professor of law at Harvard University.

Chapter 6

Simon and Schuster: Selling Bigotry

Simon and Schuster Backs Carter's Falsehoods

By Andrea Levin

In the controversy over Jimmy Carter's error-ridden book *Palestine: Peace Not Apartheid,* the role of publisher Simon and Schuster has been largely ignored. The assumption, evidently, is that a company producing, promoting and profiting from a supposedly "non-fiction" history on a contentious topic bears no responsibility whatsoever for the book's accuracy—or falsity.

Indeed, Simon and Schuster makes little pretense of assuring the factual merit of its product or of redressing misinformation when it's brought to editors' attention—unlike newspapers, for instance, whose oversight systems seek to minimize error and correct inaccuracies. It's noteworthy that, in contrast to the world of journalism, there are no book-publishing codes of ethics to promote fact-checking and accuracy for books designated as non-fiction.

Thus, the firestorm concerning Carter's falsehoods elicited no statement by the publishers proposing an overhaul of his book or even a review of it (with, say, a detailed errata sheet correcting the errors being added to copies already on library and bookstore shelves).

On the contrary, Vice President of Corporate Communications Adam Rothberg told *Publishers Weekly* when asked whether S&S will change the book: "We're going to stick with the president's version." Similarly, in a phone conversation with CAMERA on the subject, he said: "It's Carter's book." That is, Simon and Schuster is not responsible or accountable.

Simon and Schuster publisher David Rosenthal was even more dismissive. After Kenneth Stein, former executive director of the Carter Center, resigned as a fellow of the Center, deploring the "factual errors, copied materials not cited, superficialities, glaring omissions and simply invented segments" in the work, Rosenthal declared: "We're confident in the book." He added: "Do we check every line in every book? No, but that's not the issue here. I have no reason to doubt Carter's research." (*New York Times,* December 7, 2006)

Rosenthal told the *Los Angeles Times:* "We haven't seen these allegations, we haven't seen any specifics," adding "and I have no way of assessing anything he [Stein] has said.... This is all about nothing. We stand behind the book fully, and the fact that there has been a divided reaction to it is not surprising."

Carter himself has insisted his book was carefully fact-checked. A December 8, 2006 CNN story reports his having said he "fact-checked the book with a prominent Middle East journalist and an Emory University history professor, who also works at the Carter Center." Who the journalist is remains unclear, but the same day, a story in the Emory student paper reported: "Steven Hochman, director of research and assistant to President Carter, worked with college senior Alexandra Brodman to do fact-checking and basic research for Carter's book, but did not participate in writing the book."

Hochman's academic focus is the American presidency and U.S. history. Brodman, a former intern at the Carter Center, majored in Japanese and international affairs. Neither, that is to say, has expertise in the subject of the book. Nor, it's obvious, did they actually fact-check.

The former president has publicly conceded just one point, acknowledging that a passage was "worded in a completely improper and stupid way," suggesting terrorism against Israel might legitimately continue until that nation met Carter's prescriptions for peace. According to Professer Melvin Konner, that "sentence, simply put, makes President Carter an apologist for terrorists and places my children, along with all Jews everywhere, in greater danger." The former president said he's asked his publisher to change the wording in future editions of his book.

Simon and Schuster has, however, made clear it has no intention of addressing the avalanche of comment citing other factual problems. On January 23, 2007, CAMERA provided a detailed list of factual errors to Adam Rothberg urging corrections. No response has yet been received.

The *Business* of Publishing

The publishing industry's general laxity in vetting for accuracy in non-fiction works does lead to embarrassments such as the case of another Simon & Schuster "non-fiction" book from 2003. *Honor Lost* turned out to be an invented story of a Jordanian honor killing victim. Multiple errors were quickly spotted by Jordanian women's rights activists who disputed the book's central premise about the alleged victim in question as well as myriad smaller errors.

However, an S&S statement by Adam Rothberg said author Norma Khouri provided "satisfactory responses to the matters raised," and "nothing indicated to us or Random [House, which published the book in Australia,] that her work was fiction." Several errors were corrected, but a paperback edition went forward with the bogus story.

When a persistent journalist, after 18 months of research, finally unmasked the fraud for all to see, the book was withdrawn from stores; 50,000 had been sold in the U.S. and 200,000 in Australia. The hesitation to act on the Khouri case—as in that of Carter's book—is clearly financial. Errors of fact may be nettlesome at times in terms of negative publicity, but only occasionally rise to the level of major scandal sufficient to jeopardize sales. For instance, *Palestine: Peace Not Apartheid* ranked on the *New York Times* best seller list for more than a dozen weeks.

If alien abduction is considered "evidence-based" at Simon and Schuster, can anyone be shocked that Jimmy Carter's publisher sees no problem with his ludicrous rendition of the Arab-Israeli conflict.

According to a December 2006 story in the *Times,* Carter's book had "sold nearly all of the 310,000 copies in its initial printing" and "the company has since pushed the number in circulation to 675,000." (Ironically, the same story quotes Simon and Schuster's Rosenthal on the robust sales in 2006 of non-fiction books, saying: "If there's any theme to the year it's that people only want to read the truth.")

Commenting on the publishing industry in the *Columbia Journalism Review* (July/August 1991), Professor Steve Weinberg of the Missouri School of Journalism remarked on "Publishing's dirty secret," that "inaccuracies abound" and little concern is shown by the industry:

> Trade publishing is a for-profit endeavor; spending money for fact-checking would cut into profits. Moreover, few readers pay attention to which publishers are responsible and which are not; for whatever reasons, there is little brand-recognition among consumers of books. Many consumers are aware that the *National Enquirer* is an unreliable newspaper, but they have no idea which book publishers are the industry's *National Enquirer* equivalents.

Yet, he argues, there are solutions. Trade publishers "could pay in-house or outside researchers to request documentation from the author, then judge its worthiness. At the very least, they could pay for a spot check, then decide whether a full-scale review is necessary. (Models already exist in university presses, which traditionally send manuscripts to two or more outside readers knowledgeable in the subject area, paying those readers a stipend for their documented opinion.)"

In a 1998 *Baltimore Sun* article ("The shame of publishing: Truth is of no concern"), Weinberg recounted that Simon and Schuster had just published *The Threat: The Secret Alien Agenda,* in which the author claimed "that behind the countless number of alien missions to abduct Earthlings is a plot to control the planet by breeding the citizenry to become a different kind of species."

The S&S Web site today still touts this book as "the first evidence-based explanation of a mystery that has perplexed scientists for decades" and calls it "a direct, authoritative challenge to researchers who believe the abduction phenomenon is essentially benevolent and spiritually uplifting..."

If alien abduction is considered "evidence-based" at Simon and Schuster, can anyone be shocked that Jimmy Carter's publisher sees no problem with his ludicrous rendition of the Arab-Israeli conflict. The calumnies in *Palestine: Peace Not Apartheid* are, of course, no joke, and their potential for poisoning public understanding of the complex Middle East is truly troubling. The cavalier attitude of the company in defaming Israel should awaken the public to the reality that there major publishers who purvey the most outlandish fiction as fact and their products should be treated accordingly.

Reform of this shoddy industry can't begin too soon—especially in light of the impending publication by Farrar, Straus and Giroux of a book version of Professors Stephen Walt and John Mearsheimer's error-laden screed on the so-called "Israel Lobby."

Andrea Levin is Executive Director of CAMERA.

An Open Letter to Simon and Schuster and CEO Jack Romanos

Peace Can't Be Built on A Foundation of Lies

Correct Carter's Falsehoods

All those who seek an enduring Israeli-Palestinian settlement must be dismayed by former President Jimmy Carter's error-riddled book, *Palestine: Peace Not Apartheid.* In falsely casting Israel as a malevolent, colonialist power overwhelmingly responsible for failed peace efforts, Carter encourages those who obstruct resolution of the conflict and pursue Israel's annihilation.

We urge a full and systematic review of the book and public correction of every material error. Below are a few of the many untruths. Others can be found at www.camera.org —

CARTER SAYS –

P. 57 **The 1949 armistice demarcation lines became the borders of the new nation of Israel and were accepted by Israel and the United States, and recognized officially by the United Nations.**

P. 215 **[An option for Israel is] withdrawal to the 1967 border specified in U.N. Resolution 242 and as promised in the Camp David Accords and the Oslo Agreement...**

THE FACTS

- Carter repeats many times variations on these falsehoods about Israel's borders and the contents of U.N. Security Council Resolution 242. Contrary to Carter, 242 does not require Israel's returning to the pre-1967 lines. Lord Caradon, an architect of the resolution, said, "It would have been wrong to demand that Israel return to its positions of June 4, 1967, because those positions were undesirable and artificial. After all, they were just the places where the soldiers of each side happened to be on the day the fighting stopped in 1948. They were just armistice lines. That's why we didn't demand that the Israelis return to them."
- Israel's only international borders are those with Jordan, Egypt and Lebanon. The 1949 armistice lines separating the West Bank from Israel never became permanent borders recognized by Israel, the United States or the U.N. Security Council. Resolution 242 requires negotiations to resolve the ultimate designation of that boundary and those final status talks have yet to occur.

CARTER SAYS –

P. 51-52 **...[I]mportant provisions of our [1978/79] agreement have not been honored since I left office. The Israelis have never granted any appreciable autonomy to the Palestinians...**

THE FACTS

- Carter continually misrepresents facts about the Camp David agreements he oversaw, obscuring Arab responsibility for their flawed implementation. Here he omits that Palestinian autonomy as envisioned in the agreements was bitterly opposed by the very PLO he defends. Yasir Arafat and his lieutenants publicly denounced autonomy efforts and Palestinians who supported them were killed.
- Obviously, after 1993 the Palestinians gained "appreciable autonomy." The Oslo process created the Palestinian Authority and gave Palestinians control of political, civic, security, medical, educational and media institutions. Israel ceded 40% of the West Bank and evacuated the entire Gaza Strip. Any subsequent Israeli military incursions into these areas have been in response to their use by Palestinians as bases for terrorism.

CARTER SAYS –

P. 62 **When I met with Yasir Arafat in 1990, he stated, "The PLO has never advocated the annihilation of Israel. The Zionists started the 'drive the Jews into the sea' slogan and attributed it to the PLO."**

THE FACTS

- Carter often quotes as fact, without any qualification, such baseless statements by Israel's adversaries. The PLO's founding charter contains multiple demands for the elimination of Israel, and Arafat himself frequently called for destroying that nation, as in: "Peace for us means the destruction of Israel. We are preparing for an all-out war, a war which will last for generations." (February 1980) Other PLO leaders have also demonized Israel, urging jihad against and elimination of the Jewish state.

CARTER SAYS –

P. 190 **The governments of Ariel Sharon and Ehud Olmert have built the fence and wall entirely within Palestinian territory, intruding deeply into the West Bank to encompass Israeli settlement blocs and large areas of other Palestinian land.**

THE FACTS

- This too is erroneous. United Nations numbers confirm that the barrier under construction directly follows 45% of the "green line," the 1949 Armistice Line. Clearly the "green line" is not "within Palestinian territory." Those areas where the barrier deviates east of the line are, according to 242, disputed areas yet to be negotiated. Moreover, in some places the barrier also veers into Israeli territory.
- So extreme is Carter's hostility to Israel that he ignores the effectiveness of the structure in thwarting lethal attacks and saving lives. Israeli fatalities have decreased by 70% since construction of the barrier.

Simon and Schuster has, regrettably, fueled bias and prejudice in publishing Carter's screed with its innumerable factual errors.

Now is the time to set the record straight.

Contact Simon and Schuster and Jack Romanos at **212-698-7000.**

CAMERA®

Committee for Accuracy in Middle East Reporting in America

P.O. Box 35040
Boston, MA 02135

www.camera.org